2004 PC

ONC
A RHYME

IMAGINATION FOR
A NEW GENERATION

Essex Vol II
Edited by Steve Twelvetree

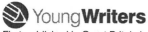 Young**Writers**

First published in Great Britain in 2004 by:
Young Writers
Remus House
Coltsfoot Drive
Peterborough
PE2 9JX
Telephone: 01733 890066
Website: www.youngwriters.co.uk

SB ISBN 1 84460 560 4

Foreword

Young Writers was established in 1991 and has been passionately devoted to the promotion of reading and writing in children and young adults ever since. The quest continues today. Young Writers remains as committed to engendering the fostering of burgeoning poetic and literary talent as ever.

This year's Young Writers competition has proven as vibrant and dynamic as ever and we are delighted to present a showcase of the best poetry from across the UK. Each poem has been carefully selected from a wealth of *Once Upon A Rhyme* entries before ultimately being published in this, our twelfth primary school poetry series.

Once again, we have been supremely impressed by the overall high quality of the entries we have received. The imagination, energy and creativity which has gone into each young writer's entry made choosing the best poems a challenging and often difficult but ultimately hugely rewarding task - the general high standard of the work submitted amply vindicating this opportunity to bring their poetry to a larger appreciative audience.

We sincerely hope you are pleased with our final selection and that you will enjoy *Once Upon A Rhyme Essex Vol II* for many years to come.

Contents

Maryan Abdikarim (10)   19
Aran James May (11)   20
Sirita Kaur (10)   20
Naila Chohan (10)   21
Eman Saleh (11)   21
Sadia Kalam (8)   22
Shakera Chowdhury (11)   22
Afshah Mumtaz (10)   23
Khadeeja Khanom (11)   23
Elisha Kaur Sahota (10)   24
Liam Chai (11)   25
Alia Banafunzi (10)   25
Devan Dave (11)   26
Manpreet Riyat (11)   26
Sabah Mahmood (11)   27
Rabeha Malik (11)   27
Mica Ashton (11)   28
Gursharn Bassi (8)   28
Tehreem Javaid (8)   29
Rabia Asif (11)   30

Coopersale & Theydon Garnon CE Primary School

Jack Pretlove-Redmond (11)   30
Luke Mallison (11)   31
Shane Morris (11)   32
Jed Bouchareb (10)   33
Elliott Billings (10)   34
Anna Pitts (11)   35
Joshua Townshend (10)   36
Georgia Barker (11)   36
Cameron Furlong (11)   37
James Hatch (11)   37
Megan Lawton (11)   38
Rae Leadley (10)   39
David Dyster (11)   40
Lucy Burkin (11)   41
Claire Broadbent (11)   42
Joe Harris (11)   43
Thomas Salter (11)   44
George Perry (11)   45
Sam Needham (10)   46

Grove Primary School

Leanne Sands (10)	65
Ellis Tucker (9)	65
Reaghan Hearn (10)	66
Anisa Jaman (9)	66
Harry Glassgow (10)	67
Luke Shepherd (9)	67
Luke Roberts (9)	68
Lee Palmer (10)	68
Holly Trimby (10)	69
Arran Sharma (10)	69
Louise Burgess (10)	70
Georgia Louise Stone (10)	70
Falina Maisuria (9)	71
Sean Thomas (10)	71
Caitlin McDonnell (9)	72
Haris Jabbar (9)	72
Zahra Khan (10)	73
Arun Sharma (9)	73
Djamel Chaalal (9)	74
David Sohal (10)	74
Erin Clover Robinson (9)	74
Amy Wood (9)	74
Gerry Oakes (10)	75
Michael Bolton (10)	75
Thanusheeyaa Santhiramathirvan (8)	75
Bobby Lomas (9)	75

Hazelmere County Junior School

Cathy Clewley (11)	76
Delanie Blastock (10)	76
Hannah Underwood (8)	77
Katie Stevens (11)	77

Holland Park Primary School

Kimberley Davies (11)	77
Charley Manners (10)	78
James Bettis (10)	78
Sam Seago (11)	79
Sarah Allerton (10)	79
Olivia Burfoot (10)	80
Amber Watts (10)	80

Georgia Hickey (9)	81
Oliver Will (10)	81
Ian Porter (10)	82
Christopher Gadeke (10)	82
Chris Wilson (11)	83
Eddie Parsons (11)	83
Hannah Baker (11)	84
Kelly Holdbrook (11)	84
Faye Walton (11)	85
Clare Gravatt (10)	85
Sam Mahoney (11)	86
Harry Ryan (10)	86
Kyle Lowis (10)	87
Liam Torr-Clark (10)	87
Hannah Needham (9)	88
Matthew Cross (10)	88
Thomas Moodey (8)	89
Laura Vile (9)	89
Daniel Fairbanks (8)	90
Thomas Wilkinson (10)	90
Kirsty Muir (10)	91
Ava Pickett (10)	91
Luke Elkes (10)	92
Jonah Lees (8)	92
Louise Rodwell (11)	93
Louis Lavallin (10)	93
Lydia Hills (10)	94
Megan Ganderton (9)	94
Bethany (8)	95
Francesca Dulieu (8)	95
Stefanie Klarner (11)	96
Courtney Eastman (9)	96
Adam Gardiner (11)	97
James Smart (11)	97
Natalie Creelman (11)	98
Gemma Day	98
Emily Gallone (10)	99
Claire Hills (10)	99
Robert McNair Wilson (11)	100
Jonathan Strutt (11)	100
Laura Gilbert (11)	101
Georgina Woolfe (11)	101

William Anderson-White (11)   102
Aaron Redpath (11)   102

Holly Trees Primary School
Lauren Heron (7)   103
Emilie Cobb (9)   103
Sophie Drew (11)   104
Lauren Gregory & Megan Tuck (10)   104
Sarah Anne Brialey (9)   105
Danielle Carr (11)   105
Amy Simmonds (8)   106
Jake Wallace (11)   106
Suelen Tenn (8)   107

Holly Trinity CE Primary School
Bernadette Rees (11)   108
Natalie Fisher (11)   109
Jordan Brown (10)   109
Melissa Godfrey (10)   110
Elizabeth Barron (11)   111
Daniel Morris (10)   112
Alex McKenzie (11)   113
Amber Callaghan (10)   114
Luke Gosney (11)   114
Lauren Britton (10)   115
Christopher King (11)   115
Natasha Lamont (11)   116
Lee Moffat (11)   116
Lucy Phillips (10)   117
Shaun Warren (11)   117
Lindsey Marsh (11)   118
David Weir (11)   118
Robert Scott (10)   119
Bradley Mason (11)   119
Hannah Suttling (11)   120
Keeley Bell (11)   121
Amy Suttling (11)   122
Linzi White (11)   123
Lauren Henderson (11)   124

Maldon Primary School

Joy Young (10)	124
James-Morgan Dee (10)	125
Charlotte Johnson (10)	125
Tom Willey (11)	126
Lauren Connolly (9)	126
Jessica Waterman (11)	127
Fleur Young (10)	127
Daniel Billing (11)	128
Iain Buchanan (8)	128
Sam Jeffries (11)	129
Grace Highton (11)	129
George Jones (9)	129
Aaron South (11)	130

Melbourne Park Primary School

Aidan Moore (7)	130
Lucy Bearcroft (7)	131
Christopher McDonald (8)	131
Katie Williams (7)	131
Latoya Smith (11)	132
Ryan Moore (8)	132
Holly Rainbird (10)	133
Stephanie Giarnese (8)	133
Sharrel Devenish (8)	134
Tayla Peel (7)	134
Lorna Dunn (8)	134
Paige Harlow (10)	135
Jordan Brown (7)	135
Josh Ripton (7)	135
Reece Babij (8)	136
Claire Barker (7)	136
Demi Elles (10)	136
Poppe Johnson (10)	137
Nicola Peters (10)	137
Nyomie Vaughan (11)	137
Michael Hunt (10)	138
Scott Bond (9)	138
Liam Fitzgeorge (8)	138
Danni Walsh (10)	139
Kelly Stratford (11)	139

William Prince (9)	139
Steven Cox (10)	140
Joshua Kendall (10)	140
Andrew Blanc (10)	140
Aaron Khadbai (8)	141
Keeley Hull (9)	141
Bradley Daly	141
Liam Smith (8)	142
Charlotte Foster (8)	142
George Chittock (8)	142
Amill-Mal Rourke (9)	143
Edson Clarke (10)	143
Jenny Carter (11)	143
Abigail Loble (9)	144
Louiscia McLeod (8)	144
Shannon O'Toole (10)	145
Emma Bearcroft (9)	145
Danielle Stimpson (10)	146
Sarah Gruneberg (11)	146
Jack Ryan (10)	147
Levi-Wayne Stanley (7)	147
Ahmed Karim (10)	147
Ellie Rose Folkard (8)	148
Ben Hastings (11)	148
Leah Kirby (9)	149
Jade Turner (10)	149
Harry Sharp (9)	150
Jonathon Russell (9)	150
Katie Turner-Wright (9)	150
Mary-Louise Harrington (9)	151
Naomi Toublic (9)	151
Curtis Devenish (9)	152

Millfields Primary School

Claudia Sandford-Bates (10)	152
Emily Hirst (10)	153
George Fisher (10)	153
Harriet Scott (10)	154
Charlotte Fern Bryan (10)	154
James Coppin (7)	155
Thomas Liddy (8)	155

Chelsea Duce (10)   156
Alex Tierney (9)   156
Hannah Nelson (10)   157
Matty Duce (8)   158
Robbie Taylor Hunt (10)   158
Laurel Regibeau (8)   159
Louisa Theeman (7)   159
Alfred Twyman (7)   160
Bill Twyman (10)   160
Miriam Clavane (8)   161
James Blanchette (8)   161
Mia Krikler (8)   162
Petra Jones (10)   162
Rebecca Hart (7)   163
Chippy Clarke (10)   163
Dayle Martyn Foreman (10)   164
Tom Connery (8)   164
Jake Toby Hughes (10)   165
Samuel Williamson (8)   165

Northwick Park Junior School

Emma O'Neill (9)   165
Hollie-Ann Boomer (10)   166
Roni Louise Foyster (9)   166
Faye Rogers (9)   167
Connar Hobbs (11)   167
Shannon Mostyn (10)   168
Ellis Evans (9)   168
Jessica Bronze (10)   169
Jessica Nelson (10)   170
Michaela Bannon (8)   170
Bethany Barnard (9)   171
Jessica Andrews (9)   171
Amy Hadden (10)   172
Holly Barlow (10)   172
Elisha Brett (9)   173
Leesha Louise Goody (11)   173
Georgia Louise Dean (11)   173
Thomas Daykin-Woodberry (11)   174
James Cory (10)   174
Kara-Anne Johnston (10)   175

Jordan Parsons (8)	175
Molly Minton (8)	176
Paige Quinn (10)	176
Aaron Holmes (8)	176
Molly Rose-Smith (11)	177
Sophie Edwards (9)	177
Danielle Winter (10)	177

Old Heath Primary School

Kori Learoyd Tuckwell	178
Holly Lewis	178
Chloe Pudney	179

Prettygate Junior School

Autumn Tidmarsh (9)	179
Oliver Totham (10)	180
Alex Sutcliffe (9)	180
Taras Kokolski (10)	181
Charlotte Graves (9)	181
Amy Ketley (10)	182
Emily Jackson (10)	182
Alice Fawkes (9)	183
Alexander Hindle (10)	183
Dale Gladwin (9)	183
Anna Walker (9)	184
Maryam Nadim (9)	184
Daniel Whitmore (10)	185
Jemma Whitmore (9)	185
Holly Sibley (8)	186
Nathanael Dale (10)	186
James Bouckley (9)	187
Mathew Streeting (10)	187
Abbie Alpine (9)	188
Elizabeth Hampshire (10)	188
Nathan Courtier (8)	189
Joshua Wright (10)	189
Rachael Garnham (9)	189
Amy Louise Eavery (9)	190
Rebecca Kelker (9)	190
Jade Norris (8)	190
Julian Chamberlain-Carter (10)	191

Michael Nugent (10)	209
Laura North (10)	210
Megan Rogers (11)	210
Nicola Horridge (10)	211
Cherise O'Sullivan (11)	211
Jessica Harrison (11)	212
George Ebert (10)	212
Tommy Unwin (10)	213
Amy Chessher (10)	213
Carl Harrison (11)	214
Siân O'Sullivan (7)	214
Amy Sands (10)	215
Lewis Rix (11)	215
Demi Mills (10)	216
Jessica Samuel (10)	216
Billie Kennerson (11)	217
Toby Moore (8)	217
Aaron Parsons (9)	218
Alfie Ryan (10)	218
Sophie Jenkins (8)	219
Georgia Smith (9)	219
Rebecca Green (9)	219
Luke Abrahams (11)	220
Lewis Winters (7)	220
Kailey Bickmore (9)	221
Billy Markham (9)	221
Rebecca Boyce (9)	222
Bethan Gully (7)	222
Anthony Martin (11)	223
Clara-Jane Edwards (10)	223
James Coburn (10)	224
Sophie Andrews (8)	224
Ellie Noble (8)	224
Michael Wilks (9)	224
Meg Barry (9)	225
Samuel Webster (9)	226
Jade Carey (10)	227
Joe O'Neill (11)	227
Jessica Irvine (9)	228
Michaela Black (11)	228
Amber Edwards (11)	229

The Poems

Creatures

If you're brave and daring
Climb up the misty peak
And there you'll find a dragon
Baring its glossy teeth.

If you're brave and daring
Climb the rocky caves
And there you'll find a cyclops
Who hasn't slept for days.

If you're brave and daring
Climb the tallest tower
And there you'll find some bats
Who hang around for hours.

If you're brave and daring
Among the snowy rocks
There you'll find a yeti
Scaring human flocks.

If you're brave and daring
Enter the castle of doom
And there you'll find some witches
Casting a spell on you.

Hollie Barden (11)
Benhurst Primary School

Prince Cinders

A man so small,
With no family to adore,
Sits alone,
Scrubbing the floor.

A man so bonny,
So weak, so small,
Sits washing the socks,
He's not loved at all.

His brothers don't care,
They leave him alone,
To do all the work,
All on his own.

Prince Cinders is his name,
Can you believe he's a prince?
He's spotty, so skinny,
He's the most unbelievable of them all.

Mistura Yusuf (10)
Benhurst Primary School

War

War is children not wanting their parents to leave.
War is people hungry, starving, wanting food.
War is people fighting, attacking and bombing each other.
War is people dying, people getting killed.

Rose Shalloo (10)
Benhurst Primary School

The Dolphin Dance

When the clocks strike midnight
The dolphins leap
One for joy
One for luck.

Springing out the ocean
The stars lighting their way
Nothing there to stop them
That's the dolphins' life.

When they reach the valley
They rest a while in peace
Nibbling on the seaweed
Drinking the salty sea.

When the sun arises
The dolphins turn back
And return back to the bay
That's how the dolphins live.

Zoe Schafer (11)
Benhurst Primary School

Rainforest Unearthed!

Asking for its own detail,
An entire piece of unsearched land,
Being burnt, crushed and ruined,
Has never truly been found.

Does any poor soul realise
Hopeless extinctions lie low in disguise?
Poor innocent animals lose their mind
Because of cruel and selfish mankind.

Sadly the unearthed rainforest
Lives to grimly die,
And all we are doing is saying
A larger goodbye!

Francoise Macaly (11)
Cleveland Junior School

Missing Someone

I'm missing my somebody,
Without them I can't live happily,
No one can be me,
Not even if they wanted to be.

When I'm sad I write and sing,
Remembering my someone giving me a ring.
My someone gave me a watch,
I love them all so much.

Strength is something hard to build,
But my someone's love covers bad like a shield.
Life is not all bad,
I'm just feeling a little sad.

I keep my faith,
That's why I feel so safe.
No matter what,
My love for somebody is a lot.

This poem is about me,
Missing my family.

Zakiyah Ahmed (11)
Cleveland Junior School

Rainforest

I am very hot
But sometimes I'm cold.
I can be noisy
But never quiet.
I am dark at the bottom
But bright at the top.
I can always be dangerous.
I will play sometimes but not at dark.
I have lots of colours in me.

What am I?

Rainforest.

Qaisar Ahmed (11)
Cleveland Junior School

Guess Who?

A song gallery
Plastic surgery
Not so fat
Dances with a hat
Bleached his face
Is he a disgrace?
Child lover
The unblack brother
Used to have an afro
Now called a wacko
A court dodger
No lodger
Lives in Neverland
Near the sea and sand
A calm voice
And the limo of his choice
Loves up his suits
With the gold and white boots
When he moonwalks up the stage
His fans get engaged.

Answer: Michael Jackson

Charlie Bowers (11)
Cleveland Junior School

What Am I?

I have lots of colour
I am dark at the bottom and light at the top
I often make a lot of noise
I am never lonely
I am very big
I have lots of animals
I am always dying.

What am I?

Benjamin Francis
Cleveland Junior School

Bye-Bye Houllier

Houllier could get sacked,
He'd better start getting packed.
He calls himself a boss,
But really he's at a loss.

Kenny Dalglish is hopefully coming,
Then maybe we'll start running
And possibly even win
Then we'll start to sing:
'You'll never walk alone . . .'

Some Thailand geezer might be coming,
Well, at least, he's better than nothing.
(That's what Houllier is right now)
He won us a cup, I don't know how!

This is it, he's gone somehow,
Bonjour was then, au revoir is now.

Mubariz Karim (11)
Cleveland Junior School

Who Am I?

I am beautiful and colourful,
I live in the rainforest,
I eat fruits,
I can do a thing that no other animal can,
I am famous for it,
I also sometimes live in houses, but in a cage,
But some people don't trust me because I give their secrets away,
I am not a mammal and not an amphibian,
But I am a vertebrate.

What am I?

Pradeep Joalex Jerome (11)
Cleveland Junior School

What's The Story In The Beautiful Rainforest?

Is this the life?
Oh! Is this the life?
Trees blowing wind to me,
I feel like I am a flea.
Parrots flying in the sky,
I wish I could fly.
Caterpillar crawling on the leaves,
If there were no sun I would freeze.
Frogs leaping across the pond,
I think I am really getting fond.
Snakes slither around my body,
All the animals are not that goody.
Monkeys swing tree to tree,
It's like I am a bird that is free.
Jaguar running to catch its prey,
If you feel tired you have to lay.
Arrow poison frog is waiting to be poisoned,
Don't trying catching one because you will be poisoned.
People wandering around the forest,
I'm not sure if they would have a rest.
Is this the life?
Oh! Is this the life?
I feel free,
The breeze is waiting for me.

Pathushani Ganeshan (11)
Cleveland Junior School

Guess Who?

The forest is dark
Where all the animals live
Plants are shivering
Animals are done
Plants are shivering around them
Ready for them . . . go!

Liban Hussain (11)
Cleveland Junior School

I'm Alone

I'm alone! I'm alone!
I've been like this for sixty-five years,
All old with no friends,
The green, sparkling trees around me laugh and stare,
I search for friends, but everyone ignores me.
I wish I wasn't alone, very alone.

Humans, why are you so mean?
You use me to cure you while you do the opposite to me,
You use me as a toilet,
You climb me - it hurts,
Bullets hit me - they kill,
You're the reason why I'm alone.

Little creatures, why do you tickle me?
You also take me away leaf by leaf.
Bees, you always sting me as you make a home in me,
Monkeys, you hurt me the most,
You swing on me - it really hurts.
The message I have to say is, *'Stop it!'*

Avneet Uppal (11)
Cleveland Junior School

The Calm Sea

The tame, wild wind is calm.
As the swirling, soft sea makes them go to sleep.
The small stars gleam onto the blue sea to form a beautiful reflection.
As the wind swirls and swirls, the only, calm sea forms small,

soft caves.

The calm sea rests.
At night the sea turns dark and the pulsing beat of the waves.
Lonely fishes searching for food in the calm sea.
Exotic creatures of the sea go to sleep.
As the hours tick by, day starts and creatures come back to life.

Sabha Mahmood (8)
Cleveland Junior School

Life Without Rain

Under the hot, scorching sun,
The people of Africa look up to the cloudless sky
Imagining life with rain.

Green crops would grow,
Animals roaming in the fields,
Children growing and happily playing,
Shoes, protecting the blistered feet from the ground
And worries left so far behind.

But life is without rain,
Where people are starving and die of hunger.
Children crying and confused,
Feet rubbing against the hard ground in search of water
With no result found.

Water is precious
And would bring hope to many people that need it
But do not receive it.
Imagine life without water . . .
Imagine . . .

Rizwan Nasrullah (10)
Cleveland Junior School

Eyes Of The Rainforest

As you seek the rainforest, quiet soon comes,
But then again you hear the slow thump of tribal drums.
Within the thickness of the rainforest you'll soon find,
Gleaming eyes here, there and behind.

Trees fall and a new cycle starts,
Fruits of nature are separated in parts.
Ways of the rainforest a light sight,
The warm, steam air a delicious bite.

Jetal Odedra (11)
Cleveland Junior School

What Is It In The Rainforest?

Long liver,
Doesn't shiver,
Good loser,
Big dozer,
Non-speaker,
Food seeker,
Good swimmer,
Bad grinner,
Isn't a talker,
Slow walker,
Is prey,
Doesn't say,
Has shell,
Doesn't smell.

Suhaib Rafiq (11)
Cleveland Junior School

Rainforest!

Long liver
Doesn't shiver
Non-speaker
Bad grinder
Sick player
Bad joker
Bad pretender
Long lanky
Very shanky
Very dirty
Get very leary.

Rashed Mirza (11)
Cleveland Junior School

Rainforest Journey

Green leaves shooting out,
Birds flying all about,
Monkeys swinging tree to tree,
Buzz goes the bumble bee.

Hiss goes the slithery snake,
As the spider drowns in lake,
Insects are running round,
Jaguars being very proud.

Piranhas are eating flesh,
Alligators are getting fresh,
Parrots screeching at the tree top,
Fishes jump then always drop.

Green leaves shooting out,
Birds flying all about,
Monkeys swinging tree to tree,
Buzz goes the bumble bee!

Sruthy Harilal (10)
Cleveland Junior School

Guess What I Am?

I have a beak
A long one too
Beautiful feathers
And a nice peach tongue
I like lizards
But I also love fruits
I have long claws
And a black and white face.

Take a lucky guess . . .
What am I?

Elizabeth Ajayi (11)
Cleveland Junior School

Rainforests

Green leaves everywhere
Also red and yellow too.
Insects seeking
Through and through
For a comfy spot to sleep.
Tomorrow is another journey.

Green swamps everywhere
Also blue and yellow too.
Fishes swimming,
Slick and fast
Through the colourful
Coral reefs.

Brown branches everywhere
Also light brown too.
Birds flying
Silently and mysteriously
Over the dark blue
Night sky.

Monica Malik (11)
Cleveland Junior School

Snake

Slippy slider
Quiet hider
Animal killer
Human swallower
Poison squirter
Jaw opener
Dangerous creature
Slimy things
Slippery reptiles
Long and longer

Sssssss . . .

Zohra Asim (11)
Cleveland Junior School

Rainforests!

I hear the sound of monkeys,
Ooh ah ah.
The rustle of the leaves,
Shimmer, shimmer,
Shimmer.

Herd of animals,
Quiver, quiver, quiver.
Looking for directions,
No idea where to go.

I'm so stuck,
Help me, I've got no luck!

Ooh ah ah,
Shimmer, shimmer, shimmer.
Herd of animals.
Quiver, quiver, quiver.

To describe the rainforest,
It's damp,
Dark,
Bright,
It's humid as well
But I'd stay there all night!

Mehvish Arshad (10)
Cleveland Junior School

Walk Through The Rainforest

The forest is dark,
The leaves are green.
Snakes are slithering around me.
Owls are howling on top of the trees.
Bees are buzzing all around me.
The monkeys always giggle,
Their tails always wiggle,
That's why we're always tickled!

Bakhtawar Sethi (11)
Cleveland Junior School

Rainforest Noises

I was walking through the rainforest
Guess what I saw?
Yeah! I saw an ant
And many more.

I heard an animal
I went nearer and nearer
And don't worry
It was only my friend Sarah.

I went past the bush
I went past the trees
And there I saw a . . .
Bumble bee!

I could taste the plants and flowers
I saw a cobra
With a lot of power
I saw a chameleon
It was one out of a million.

Fatima Ahmed (11)
Cleveland Junior School

My Baby Brother

There is a new addition in the family.
Every time I try to go to sleep
He would want to cry loudly.
I try to pick him up soundly
But he refuses proudly.
I feed him happily,
Then he goes to sleep nicely.
He wakes up quickly
And wants his milk quickly,
So he can have his rest nicely.

Awais Khurseed (8)
Cleveland Junior School

Playground Rap

The gossip of the girls,
The football twirls.
The ringing of the bells,
The tasty smells.
This is kids world,
The way we live!

The teachers' moans,
Kids eating ice cream cones.
Boys have passion,
Girls have fashion.
This kids world,
The way we live!

Wild in the jungle,
We are in a bungle.
Bringing toys,
Which make *noise! noise! noise!*
This is kids world,
The way we live!

Selviya Yesmin & Nalia
Cleveland Junior School

School Is Ace!

School is a perfect base,
It is my favourite place.
When it is playtime, I have a race,
But we can't play for long, we have to haste.
One time I tripped over my lace,
And fell flat on my face!
My teacher's name is Miss Ace,
We think she is from space!
We learn at a steady pace,
Maths is the subject of my taste.
My time in school I never waste,
School is my favourite place.

Rehan Nasrullah (8)
Cleveland Junior School

Deer

Here I am
Walking quietly through the forest,
I hear a rustling from the bushes.

Wondering what it might be
I stand still.
Like a mysterious shape

I see a dark shadow.
Then a deer emerges
Silently, like a mole from the dark
Into the sunlight.

Its skin sparkling like diamonds
It gazes at me.
I move and the deer, startled,
Leaps away.
Suddenly I feel lonely.

Sam Quirk (9)
Cleveland Junior School

Rainforest!

Long liver
Doesn't shiver
Big dozer
Good loser
Non-speaker
Heavy weeper
Smells bad
Very sad
Good swimmer
Bad grinner.

Omar Defreitas (10)
Cleveland Junior School

King Of Kings

Galloping as fast as light,
Proud ruler, proud ruler.
His name is Mr Red Deer Stag,
King of all the kings.

Searching for her jewelled child,
Pretty queen, pretty queen.
Her name is Mrs Red Deer Doe,
Mother of the clearings.

Gently brushing through the trees,
Deer herd, deer herd.
They are the dukes and duchesses,
People of the woods.

Coat red as blood with white cloud spots,
Cautious prince, cautious prince.
His name is Master Red Deer Child,
Pride of all the forest.

Ashley Chhibber (9)
Cleveland Junior School

Who Am I?

I have stripes on my body
I have fur as well.

I have a tail
And big, round eyes.

I eat other animals
I run quite fast.

I have four legs
Also quite a large body.

What am I?

Tahmin Begum (11)
Cleveland Junior School

Five Senses Of The Rainforest

I can hear the rainforest
Loud and quiet
There are many noises
Day and night.

I can see the rainforest
It's a special sight
Animals eat, sleep
And even fight.

I can touch the rainforest
With my hands and fingers
I can feel the silky spider webs
As it moves and lingers.

I can smell the rainforest
With its misty, hot air
The herbs and the plants
And the apples and pears.

I can taste the rainforest
It's not a tasty meal
But the incredible thing is . . .
The herbs that heal!

Kulsum Patel (11)
Cleveland Junior School

Our World

Everyone's talking about war.
Our eyes saying no more.
Not looking forward to tomorrow.
Cos there's too much hate and sorrow.
The world around me is falling apart.
I can feel my heart saying, 'Stop, please *stop!*'

Monjur Chowdhury (8)
Cleveland Junior School

Heaven

Heaven is a gorgeous place,
Which all humans will face.
It is like a place just full of light,
Which is a place for those who do right.

It is a place of happiness,
A place free of sadness.
The huge, white cloud flying over us,
It is a humungous light,
A huge, white kite.

Those who are wise,
Are not leading to their demise.
For they will receive the love,
Of the huge, white dove.

Sultan Khan (10)
Cleveland Junior School

The Dragon And The Knight

In the forest the dragon lay,
Very eager to find his way.
He carried his heavy feet to the poisoned pool,
A knight came and said, 'What a fool!'

The dragon landed with a thump,
The knight said, 'What a bump!'
The knight giggled
While playing his fiddle.

He went home,
He wasn't alone.
Nobody knows what happened to him,
People say his spirits lay within.

Maryan Abdikarim (10)
Cleveland Junior School

Rainforest Animals

R ainforest animals are very beautiful
A naconda snake is thick and long and
I t will gobble up its prey in one go.
N aughty he is.
F at and hairy are the big gorillas and
O n the floor they sit.
R ats are ugly creatures to some people but they still
E at and live in the rainforest.
S limy frogs swim in the swamp with
T heir poison keeping them alive from predators.

A ll animals are scared of the tiger, he's very
N aughty and bites animals.
I ts house is anywhere he likes in the jungle.
M any animals are safe in the air, like
A hummingbird and a parrot.
L ots of different animals and
S o beautiful they are.

Aran James May (11)
Cleveland Junior School

Dark Whisper

R ainforests are wonders of life,
A mazing features all around,
I n the forest, animals can be found.
N ight is fallen,
F orest animals asleep in peace,
O r the spider monkey fleeing from tree to tree.
R ainforest tribes look after the forest,
E ven the forest looks after the tribes,
S o they can all live and survive,
T hat makes the rainforest full of life!

Sirita Kaur (10)
Cleveland Junior School

The Mighty Lord Of The Jungle

The mighty lord of the jungle,
The lion, lord of all the beasts,
The hearing of this beast,
Makes everyone want to obey and stay.
'Rooaar!' he says.
The mighty lord of beats.

All the little creepers,
Obey the lord and his creatures,
With his blood-sucking teeth,
He doesn't always stick with beef,
With his furry paws,
He eats more, more and more!

In the dead of night,
He goes and has a bite.
With the buzzing, the splashing and the growling,
Nothing will be so boring
The mighty lord sleeps in the sun,
No time for fun.

Naila Chohan (10)
Cleveland Junior School

Survivor

R ainforests are full of imagination and life,
A nimals and people who hunt to survive.
I n the morning, when the sun rises, the rainforests awaken,
N ight time arrives and daytime is taken.
F antastic animals are there to see,
O r the spider monkeys swinging from tree to tree.
R unning away from spears and arrows,
E very terrified animal including birds and sparrows,
S ome tropical plants are helpful cures,
T he wonderful rainforest is beautiful and secure!

Eman Saleh (11)
Cleveland Junior School

A Cat's Prey

A cat
Sat on the window sill,
Very still,
Waiting for
A mouse to kill.
Then along
Came a mouse,
Scampering along
In the house.
The cat pounces,
The cat bounces
Onto the poor
Little mouse
That scampered
In the house . . .

Sadia Kalam (8)
Cleveland Junior School

Friends

Secret teller
Music singer
Crazy laughter
Chocolate eater!

Sun lover
Homework hater
Home time lover
Mad shopper.

Money spender
Teddy cuddler
Cheeky talker
Friends forever!

Shakera Chowdhury (11)
Cleveland Junior School

The Playground

Bim bam boom, children running mad
Bim bam boom, children being glad.
On the climbing frame, children climbing high,
And some touch the sky.
Bim bam boom, children think they're cool,
Bim bam boom, they're really fools.

In the dining hall the girl in the pretty dress,
Munches and crunches and makes a big mess.
Bim bam boom, on the benches we sit,
Bim bam boom and we play to keep fit.
Children are usually talking,
And children are usually walking.

Children kick the ball,
It hits the broken wall.
Bim bam boom, children are sad,
Bim bam boom, children are glad.
A whistle will go,
They will stand in a row.

Afshah Mumtaz (10)
Cleveland Junior School

The Rainforest

A rainforest is a place for animals,
more like a home.
Most animals come from everywhere,
especially from Rome.
Beautiful flowers grow more like a rose,
there's always birds but hardly any crows.
Everywhere around me is nothing but trees,
once I take a sniff I can smell the breeze.
I'm hoping to come back soon,
if you're coming, don't come after noon!

Khadeeja Khanom (11)
Cleveland Junior School

Fluttering Nature

Butterflies and daffodils,
Spread their wings so far.
It's unbelievable to see,
How beautiful they are.

They flutter across the sky,
They swing on the ground.
They spread the world with beauty,
Far and around.

Their grace so lovely,
They reach so high.
Their wings so dainty,
Like an angel in the sky.

They turn their heads side to side,
While in the soil they dance.
They feel their way around,
As they prance, prance, prance.

When you see the pattern,
You feel the job is done.
When you see the bright yellow,
It brings out the spring sun.

The sun is what is wanted,
The sun is what it shall be.
The butterflies and daffodils are everlasting,
For you and for me.

Elisha Kaur Sahota (10)
Cleveland Junior School

The Dead

One by one they left me, my grandpa, my grandma,
My father, my mother, my brother and my sister.
Even my cousins and relatives left me.
Each saying the same last thing before they left me.

'I will be back.'
'I will be back.'

It gave me the creeps and spooks every single night.
I dare not sleep for I fear
They will be back.
Humans become ghosts.
Ghosts become humans.

The dead will rise again!

Liam Chai (11)
Cleveland Junior School

How Do You Feel?

Sometimes you feel anger
Sometimes you feel hate
And sometimes you can't take it anymore
And really want to do something horrible
But trust me, it's not worth it
It only ever gets worse.

Sometimes you feel like you hate your life
Like you wish you were dead
I felt that way when I was small
Cried as much as a waterfall
But soon I regretted it
And some day you will too.

Alia Banafunzi (10)
Cleveland Junior School

Rumble In The Rainforest

The breeze coming in your face,
and you get tripped by your lace.
The monkeys swinging from tree to tree,
being lively as if they were free.

You can see trees all around you,
quicksand on the floor is just like glue.
Many animals sprinting across the ground,
many of them discovered or found.

The temperature
as it is so much for us lot.
The atmosphere is so weird,
the insects had so much feared.

There are so many plants,
you will be astonished at the first glance.
People in the rainforest hunting,
sometimes it is really bad because of fighting.

Damp and moisture in a rainforest,
being looked at as a kind of tourist.
I am half of the world's features,
with half of the population's creatures.

Devan Dave (11)
Cleveland Junior School

Guess Who?

I have fur
And one pair of eyes.
My nose is sensitive.
My paws are warm.
I can be small and tall.
We love to eat and drink.
We play about.
We jump around.

Answer: Dog.

Manpreet Riyat (11)
Cleveland Junior School

Rainforests Everywhere!

Rainforests, rainforests everywhere!
Rainforests, rainforests far or near!

Rainforests, rainforests everywhere!
Lots of kinds of noises to hear
Also many different things to see
I wish that in a rainforest I could be!

Rainforests, rainforests everywhere!
Rainforests, rainforests far or near!

In the north, the south, the east or west
Rainforests, they're all the best
I may sometimes get a bit of a fright
But I know it's just because there's no light!

Rainforests, rainforests everywhere!
Rainforests, rainforest far or near!

All things to see and do are fun!
Even though I can't see much sun
The rainforest world is like a new dimension
And it's much better than a literacy comprehension!

Rainforests, rainforests everywhere!
Rainforests, rainforests far or near!

Sabah Mahmood (11)
Cleveland Junior School

The Lonely Snail

I am a snail, a lonely snail,
I have no family or relatives.
I am as lonely as a lost spirit,
Other snails bully me because I am so slow.
What can I do?
I need a friend so I won't be lonely anymore.
I wish I could find a friend.

Rabeha Malik (11)
Cleveland Junior School

Sounds Of The Rainforest

Buzz, buzz go the bees
Ooh, ah-ah go the monkeys in the trees
Swish, swish goes the wind in the breeze
Scratch, scratch as the animals scratch their fleas.

Squish, squash goes the mud on the floor
Peck, peck as the woodpecker pecks and sounds like it's tapping
on a door

Twitch, twitch, see if there's anything in sight
Flap, flap as the birds take flight.

Quiet, quiet as the tiger hunts his prey
Look, look, what shall I say?
Drip, drop goes the water
Step, step, waiting for slaughter.

Mica Ashton (11)
Cleveland Junior School

Night Sky

As the moon rises up
And the stars twinkle in the dark night sky
As the moonlight shines upon the house
To show us the way.
The moon follows us wherever we go
As the stars dance on the dark sky.

As you look at the moon
It seems to smile at you.
Whenever you look at the moon
It will wave back to you.
Now don't you worry
The moon will be back
With the twinkly stars tomorrow, you see.
Bye-bye!

Gursharn Bassi (8)
Cleveland Junior School

Summer

The sun is shining,
The sky is blue.
I want to play in the sunshine with you.
There is no cloud in the sky,
Or not a drop of rain.
It's summer so let's have a game.
Summer,
Summer,
Summer is the best.
Summer is the best
Weather that we have guessed.
You can see shadows,
You can see light,
And the light is coming from the sun so bright.
You can have strawberry milkshake,
You can have apple milkshake.
You can have lots of others.
In summer the flowers grow,
This way and that way, high up and low.
Summer,
Summer,
Summer is the best.
Summer is the best,
Weather we have guessed.
The sun is shining from morning to evening,
Then it gets dark and it's time for bed.
Summer,
Summer,
Summer is the best.
Summer is the best that we have guessed.

Tehreem Javaid (8)
Cleveland Junior School

The Blues

Leave me alone,
I don't feel so good.
Leave me alone,
I feel as hard as wood.

My tummy hurts,
I don't want to shout.
Leave me alone,
This is *my* bedroom, *get out!*

I'm tired,
I want to go to bed.
Leave me alone,
I want to rest my head.

When it's calm,
I love the breeze.
Everyone's left me alone,
- They're fast asleep.

Rabia Asif (11)
Cleveland Junior School

The Sun

I can creep through a window
Creep through a door.
My rays are all powerful
They will make our skin sore.

I can make flowers die
I am a great ball of fire.
Rivers disappear
I am your heart's desire.

When I arrive
You can't ignore me.
I will be your light
But I'm also deadly.

Jack Pretlove-Redmond (11)
Coopersale & Theydon Garnon CE Primary School

The Sun

I muster up the wasps
But I can also grow crops
I rescue you from your prison
Freeing you with all my wisdom.

I'm the bully of the skies
Making the weather lie
I select my prey
Burning them every day.

There is almost no escape
Not seeing me is rare
Even when I am descended
My presence is always there.

My powers are many
They are always true
Evaporation and burning
Just to name a few.

Rain and clouds are my enemies
A clear blue sky is my friend
I am an eternal guardian
The universe I defend.

Approach me, do not dare
I shall burn your body bare
For your safety I do not care
For this is my world, my lair.

I am an illusionist
You see me rise and fall
For what you see me like
Is a giant fireball.

Luke Mallison (11)
Coopersale & Theydon Garnon CE Primary School

The Sun

I can strip people bare,
And lighten up their hair.
Or I can burn to a crisp,
And make ice cream disappear like mist.

I can make people play,
And brighten up your day.
Or I can make rivers run dry,
Then you will die.

I can make water rare,
So you should beware.
Or I can be so nice,
You will be as quiet as mice.

I sit here every day,
Watching you play.
Or I can be so hot,
You will feel like a boiling pot.

I am a fiery beast,
You will be my feast.
Or I am a great ball of fire,
Your heart's desire.

Shane Morris (11)
Coopersale & Theydon Garnon CE Primary School

The Sun

I'm high in the air,
Perching on my throne,
Looking at life form,
Hasn't it grown?

When I reach my zenith,
Shadows start to shrink,
I can hide secrets,
Which will make you think.

When I am shining,
Brightly in the sky,
People on Earth,
Are starting to fry.

Look into my fire,
And you will turn blind,
Stuck in the desert,
It's a trick of the mind.

Although I am bright,
The light has to end,
Watch me closely,
As I start to descend.

Jed Bouchareb (10)
Coopersale & Theydon Garnon CE Primary School

I, The Fiery God

I can detect dust in your houses
And attract bugs to your yellow blouses.
I can make water boil with my gleam
And form milk from ice cream.

I can draw people from the shade
And to the beach for the sea where they wade.
I can wither flowers with my shine
And make dehydrated animals whine.

I can melt all the ice lollies
And defrost frozen goods inside lorries.
I can scorch the earth and make it crack
And eat up rivers as a quick snack.

I can hover in the sky
It'll be many years until I die.
And when I finally abate
What will be the Earth's fate?

I hang in the centre of space
And I turn to find something new to face.
I hold the planets around me with my mass
And if I pulled them too close they would explode into gas.

Elliott Billings (10)
Coopersale & Theydon Garnon CE Primary School

Lord Of The Sky

I can cast warm shadows,
Warming people's skin,
But I can scorch through flesh,
And burn the soul within.

I can crawl under your door,
And disturb you from your dreams,
Or peer through the curtain crack,
When morning calls for me.

My rays of shining light,
Are the life and death of flowers,
I shine in all my glory,
Revealing all my powers.

When I am at my zenith,
I will cast your shadows stout,
But when I hover in the eve,
They are long and stretched out.

You can roam free outside,
But when it is too hot,
Beware of the mirages,
Are they there or not?

My enemies are the wind,
The clouds and the rain,
But the planets are my worshippers,
They live in my domain.

I am a friend to science,
I give everything, light and heat,
I will hide behind the clouds,
Until the next time we meet!

Anna Pitts (11)
Coopersale & Theydon Garnon CE Primary School

What Am I?

I am the king of heat
And a mirage master,
I can scorch my kingdom
And cause a disaster.

A wizard made my power
I am stronger than any,
I am the ultimate source
My powers are many.

The planets are my puppets
I hold them by my reign.
They will not dare to leave me
They do not have a brain.

For if the planets leave me
They surely will die.
I am the almighty
The one who will not lie.

Joshua Townshend (10)
Coopersale & Theydon Garnon CE Primary School

My Lazy Cat

My old, furry cat,
Lay in the summer sun.
Delicate paws cupped over her ears,
Her body too lazy to run.

Mice filling up her dreams,
As she purrs contentedly in her sleep.
Now and then bustling noises pass her,
But her eyes don't open a peep.

The breeze ruffles up her fur,
As her whiskers twitch from side to side.
Then all of a sudden she wakes from the trance,
Her eyes open wide.

Georgia Barker (11)
Coopersale & Theydon Garnon CE Primary School

The Sun

I can gleam through your window
and brighten up your room
or I don't shine in your hallway
and leave it with gloom.

I can shine on the treetops
and cause a forest fire
or I could make people
water their desire.

I can make you have fun
playing in the garden
or I could be really horrible
and make your flowers harden.

I can help
your garden grow
or I could hide behind the clouds
and not show.

Cameron Furlong (11)
Coopersale & Theydon Garnon CE Primary School

The Wind

When the wind is carrying a dandelion seed along,
It is a dolphin diving deep in the ocean.
When the wind is flickering flames in a fire,
It is a firefly buzzing sharply.
When the wind is breaking branches off a tree,
It is a horse pounding rapidly.
When the wind is making a cold draught in a house,
It is a kestrel fluttering violently.

James Hatch (11)
Coopersale & Theydon Garnon CE Primary School

The Sun

I can peep through the clouds,
like a bright yellow yo-yo.
I can watch what you're doing,
though you might not know.

I can bring out some flowers,
when the summer has arrived.
This also brings the insects,
and some butterflies.

I can force you to the beach,
when I shine at my most.
I can stop rivers flowing,
when I want to boast.

I can decide when I set,
I can choose when I rise.
This can cause lots of problems,
it comes as a surprise.

I can give you some freckles,
or bronze up your skin.
I can make you very warm,
this isn't a sin.

I can defeat the rain,
with all my might.
And if you look at me closely,
I can damage your sight.

Megan Lawton (11)
Coopersale & Theydon Garnon CE Primary School

Sunny Days

I can rise early morning
and make your day bright.
I can bring you disaster
and set you alight.

My shine makes shadows
which makes you feel tall
but my warm morning power
can make you appear small.

My beams are full of power
I am the supreme
I can destroy planet Earth
I am not a dream.

I can be stronger than them all
and the people can see me clearly, they are tall
I can boil like a kettle
and I can melt away metal.

I can go high in the sky
until I reach the very top.
soon the days go by
then the night comes to shine.

I can make people happy
I can make people sad.
I can give them a tan
and I can be really bad.

Rae Leadley (10)
Coopersale & Theydon Garnon CE Primary School

The Sun

I can dehydrate animals,
And boil your car,
Or give you a tan,
And make you go to the bar.

I can make the Earth turn light,
And make you get out a kite,
Or make it turn night,
Or blind your sight.

I can melt ice lollies,
Or make you play in the sandpit,
Or make wasps appear,
And put on your swimming kit.

I make flowers die,
I can make you suffer sorely,
Or make illusions appear,
I will then make you poorly.

You can't put me out,
So don't even try,
Because if you do,
You will die.

David Dyster (11)
Coopersale & Theydon Garnon CE Primary School

The Master Of The Sky

I am an awesome source of light
I guide you through the day
Even at night I sit and watch you play
As the moon sparkles in my way.

I can boil your tea
Or glare into your eye
I can make flowers grow
But in the heat they may die.

I'm a great ball of fire
I am your designer
I sit in the sky
Nice and high.

I will make you burn
Then you will learn
Not to mess with me
I am your master.

I am like a yellow flower
But I have more power
To light up the sky
So the light will never die.

Lucy Burkin (11)
Coopersale & Theydon Garnon CE Primary School

The Sun

I can peek through curtains
Disturbing your sleep
I can brighten up your room
Without you hearing a peep.

I can light the entire world
All day and night
I can scorch your skin
With my strong rays of light.

I can make flowers bloom
And glimmer in the sky
I can provide food for plants
Or make them shrivel and die.

I am the most powerful
That no one can ever touch
If they do dare
I will hurt them very much.

I can hang in the sky
Just like a golden key
But I can soon disappear
Just you watch and see!

Claire Broadbent (11)
Coopersale & Theydon Garnon CE Primary School

Saturday Afternoon

My best TV programmes,
Are by far definitely sport,
I really enjoy the football, pitch,
And the tennis court.

I was in the football stand,
Admiring their shiny boots,
All of a sudden I looked up,
And saw a pair of coots.

As I looked up in the air,
The ball had been kicked,
So I turned around again,
And saw the posts had been nicked.

The player kicked the ball,
Towards Brian Deane,
He got tackled by the defender,
Who happened to be Keane.

As I left the stadium,
I heard an almighty roar,
I turned around in astonishment,
And saw they'd forced a draw!

Joe Harris (11)
Coopersale & Theydon Garnon CE Primary School

The Sun

I can heat up the land
so you can play all the days.
I can scald you and hurt your eyes
with my powerful UV rays.

I can give plants what they need
rays to turn into food.
I can make them shrivel and die
while I angrily brood.

I can kill foolish men
who come too near to me.
With one wave of white-hot rays
I send them screaming towards the sea.

I can give you a tan
maybe some freckles too.
As long as you're patient
and don't need to go to the loo.

Thomas Salter (11)
Coopersale & Theydon Garnon CE Primary School

The Sun

I can shine through the sky
With my head held high.
I can dehydrate animals
And make them die.

On hot, sunny days
I can burn out rain.
On lazy beaches
I can cause your skin pain.

I can blind out the moon
If I'm late at night.
I can go in when I want
And stop your daylight.

I can be very moody
And not shine all day.
Or I can be happy
And let you play all day.

George Perry (11)
Coopersale & Theydon Garnon CE Primary School

The Sun's Power

I can melt ice in my heat
When beamed upon you
Like a strong, steady beat
Dancing to a big drum.

I can demolish snow
And devour rain
I can make bad weather go
Or I can let it stay.

I can make you see
Things that are not there
I can suck up sea
While you're swimming there.

No one will ever reach me
No one will ever dare
No one will ever besiege me
So I never have to care.

The other planets are at my reign
They follow me all day
They do not even strain
Until the darkness when they are free.

Sam Needham (10)
Coopersale & Theydon Garnon CE Primary School

The Sun

I glide across the sky
Even when I'm high.
I can scald and burn
When I turn.

I live a million miles away
But I love to come and play.
When I am in pain
I let it rain.

I can make you run and hide
Or make you play with the tide.
I can make the sea glisten
All is quiet when you listen.

I bring out the flowers
With my strong powers.
I bring out the birds and bees
Who live amongst the leafy trees.

Georgia Fradd (10)
Coopersale & Theydon Garnon CE Primary School

The Sun

I can provide you with piercing light.
or arouse you with a scary fright.
I can radiate light through the sky,
or give you skin cancer and you will die.

No one can reach me because I'm so hot,
I can even melt your favourite pot.
I can make your flowers die,
and even burn your pie.

I can make you have fun,
and even sizzle your mum.
I always have a feast,
and turn into a beast.

When I am burning,
people start learning,
why I am so tough,
and I can even burn your stuff.

Charlie Brown (11)
Coopersale & Theydon Garnon CE Primary School

Rain Poem

Splitter, splatter goes the rain
Then it all comes back again.

Hustle, bustle all around,
When I look back I see it on the ground.

Rushing flushing by my side,
I find a place to hide.

Wet and windy I stood like a flame,
I feel the heat, it's sunny again.

Sophia Malik (8)
Grove Primary School

Bullying!

Why is everyone so happy?
Why is everyone so glad?
There is nothing to be happy about
Why isn't anyone mad?
You shouldn't be happy about bullying
You shouldn't be glad about bullying
The only thing you should be about bullying is be mad!
They're right there standing like a charging bull
Ready to attack any minute
So I say stay away from bullies and bullying
As far as you can
They're like bolts of lightning ready to strike
Always waiting for their next victim
And are ready to fight.

Noor Ahmad (10)
Grove Primary School

Colours

Colours here,
Colours there,
Colour everywhere.
Everywhere you go you see colours.
Black, brown, blue and pink,
These colours make you think.
Orange, green gold and white,
How about a yellow delight?
Yellow comes from the Caribbean
Blue comes from the ocean wide.
Colours that you've never seen them,
White is the colour for a beautiful bride.
Red, grey, peach and purple,
All these colours are for you.

Danielle Howes (9)
Grove Primary School

The Playground Bully

A bully is like a charging bull
who doesn't care
for people's feelings at all.
Who doesn't mind
and doesn't care,
if they pull out people's hair.
They seem to think it's a fun game,
when they call you a name.
They make you feel
like a little blob,
mostly when
you start to sob.
They boss you around
and push you about
and scream and shout.
Never go
near a
bully.

Zara Dorman (10)
Grove Primary School

Alliteration

A hunk of ham
A bottle of beer
A buzz of bees
A drop of drink
A bowl of beans
A dish of dinner
A jar of jam
A garden of grass
A pile of plates
An order of otters
A truck of trains.

Lauren Thacker (8)
Grove Primary School

The Dog

My dog was bad
And we were sad.
We went for food
We called him dude.
I went to the vet
He chased a pet.
When we were sleeping
He was reaping.
He pulled our hair
We gave him a beer.
He got all drunk
We brought him trunks.
He was lying
We started crying.
He called our name
It started to rain.

Rapheal Jegede (9)
Grove Primary School

A School Rap

Grove's the best
It's a school where you play
And you rest
And it's the best out of the rest.

Grove is the best
Grove is the best
It is full of places to rest
Grove is the best.

Grove is the school to go to
Yes, Grove is the school
That 400 people go to.

Grove is the best.

Abdullah Lounis (9)
Grove Primary School

You Big, Fat, Horrible Bully!

You big, fat bully!
I hate, I hate you, big, fat bully.
All you did was make me cry
You know you've got to change.
You're mean, mean, mean
And very stupid, stupid.
I really, really, really hate the way you are
So please, please change
And you're *dumb, dumb and getting dumber!*

Sam Brennan (10)
Grove Primary School

Rain, Rain

Drip, drop goes the rain,
    Drip, drop again and again.
Splish, splash goes the rain,
    It drops in a puddle.
Rain, hail all in a muddle,
    Shower power heavy.
Splosh, slosh, heavy rain,
    Drop, drop goes the rain,
Drip, drop again and again.

Amy Bottom (8)
Grove Primary School

Onomatopoeia

I go in the bath and see a sponge,
Splash goes the water and drops on the sponge,
Splash, splosh and makes a mess,
Mum says, 'What's going on?'
I say nothing,
When I finish, glub, glub, glub drinks the pipe down the tube.

Rohini Soni (8)
Grove Primary School

The Scar

When I came to school,
It was playtime.
I wanted to hide in the little space.
But, in the little space I was suffering from bullies.

As I was creeping, slowly and sound,
A big giant came and grabbed my shoulder,
It felt like fire burning and it tends to get bigger and bigger.

While the giant squeezed my shoulder,
I began to get a scar.
A scar that was gradually growing and growing,
Because this big bully was being racist to me.

But when the bully started being racist to me,
That really sunk in and hurt my feelings.

I begged and begged for him to stop,
But he just shook his head and said 'No'.
I pleaded for peace but I didn't get it.
Will I ever find peace?

Michelle Ulor (9)
Grove Primary School

The Peace We Have

The spark from a match
Can make love attach
Two tender hearts alike
They will not be destroyed by a spike
We like our peace very sweet
That grows on and on like wheat
The peace that we have on Earth
That is how much peace is worth.

Joseph A Odejimi (10)
Grove Primary School

The Refugee Child

I am a refugee child
Let me in, I am hungry and thirsty
I am a refugee child
Let me in, a man is pointing a gun at me
I am a refugee child
I am poor, I have not got a family to live with
I am a refugee child
I need some money to buy some food
I am a refugee child
I need a home to stay and live
I am a refugee child
Let me in, then rain is going tip, tip, I am scared of the storm
I am a refugee child
I am poor, my mum and dad are dead in the war
I am a refugee child
Let me in.

Bhavisha Thakore (9)
Grove Primary School

Kitchen

Plap! Crack! Chop! Chop!
Goes the stew, go the veggies
When it's cooking, being cut.
Squelch! Belch! Gulp! Gulp!
Goes the dough being pressed
When it's being processed.
Scrape! Scrape! Goes the knife
Being sharpened.
Whack! Crack! Goes the eggshell
Being cracked.
Clink! Clank! Go the plates
Being stacked.
Drip! Drip! Goes the tap
Not closed.

Leveena Peter (8)
Grove Primary School

Animal Feeling Poem

My mum is like a panda
Because she is soft and cuddly.

My dad is like a gorilla
Because he is big and strong.

My cousins are like two huge monkeys
Because they make me laugh.

My other cousin is like a butterfly
Because she is a very kind and sweet girl.

My nan is like a bear
Because she always says goodnight.

My granddad is like an elephant
Because he always snores.

My uncle is like a dolphin
Because he is playful.

My cousin is like a killer whale
Because he always gives me cuddles.

Georgina Fage (9)
Grove Primary School

Alliteration

A box of butter in my kitchen
Ready to be spread.
A jug of juice in my kitchen
Ready to be drunk.
A chunk of cheese in my kitchen
Ready to be eaten.
A bunch of biscuits in my kitchen
Ready to be broken and eaten up.
A saucer of sweetcorn in my kitchen
Ready to be eaten.

Aasiya Hussain (8)
Grove Primary School

The Bully

The bully stands there looking tough
The bully stands there being rough
Picking on people here and there
Calling them names
And pulling their hair.

There stands the bully
Waiting for a victim to
Pass him by
Staring at them with
An evil eye
Knowing that his victims
Are very shy.

There stands the bully.
Why do they bully,
Can anyone tell?
Is it that their life is just plain hell?
Why do they bully?
Nobody knows.

There
Stands the bully.

Zara Dorman (10)
Grove Primary School

Alliteration

A jar of jam
A hunk of ham
A cup of coke
A bowl of beans
A chunk of cheese
A plate of pleasures
A class of children
A box of biscuits.

Mickey Little (8)
Grove Primary School

Alliteration

A hunk of ham
A jar of jam
A bunch of bananas
Can I have a can of coke?
Yes!
Oh, you are a jolly folk.
How about another hunk of ham
Or a jar of jam?
No, eat your lamb.
A pile of paper.

Mia Oakley (7)
Grove Primary School

Alliteration Poem

A group of grapes
a bunch of bananas
a mopped-up mess
a cleaning cloth
a silver saucepan
a speck of scent
a mumbling mum
a clean kitchen.

Umar Ahmad (8)
Grove Primary School

The Little Donkey

Donkey
Eating apples
Apples are so juicy!
Donkey gobbles everything up!
Tasty!

Nara Franco (9)
Grove Primary School

Pet Poem

In the lady's bedroom she kept . . .
Ten chameleons you can't find
Nine snakes that hiss at you
Eight chicks that are bright yellow
Seven ginger kittens that purr
Six hopping rabbits that thump all day
Five guinea pigs that try to escape
Four caterpillars creeping everywhere
Three lizards that stand still all the time
Two donkeys galloping here and there
And one . . . guess what?

Samantha Bailey (9)
Grove Primary School

The Bully

On my first day at school I was bullied by you.
I don't like being bullied on my first day at school.
You bullied me every day.
Would you like it if you were bullied?
You are the bullies
You throw pencils at me in class
So I would get told off.
It is a bad thing to do
I wouldn't want to be one of you.

Elvisa Bajraktari (10)
Grove Primary School

Donkey

Donkey
Standing beneath
The old, green grape tree
Along came a wasp to sting him.
'Mummy!'

Rhiannah La-Rose (8)
Grove Primary School

My Baby Sis

My baby sis
Is full of bliss
Wherever she goes
She's always on her toes
With her red hair glowing
Her love is always flowing
With her little chuckle
And a little suckle
She will feel great
And she will always have a mate
But please don't make her cry
By letting her see that cloudy sky
Now that she's one
She has a lot of fun
She's learning to walk
And starting to talk
She gets lots of toys
And makes a lot of noise
And when she sucks her dummy
She wants her mummy.

Joseph Phoenix (9)
Grove Primary School

Say No To Bullying!

Remember that you should tell
Or feel like you're in Hell.
Don't wait to be told
Don't be too bold.
Don't think you are a scared pussy cat
Because you're doing the right thing and that's that.
We are a telling school
So don't be left out to look like a fool.
So we are ready to stamp bullying out.
We will never back out.

Khayam Bashir (9)
Grove Primary School

Why Did You Leave Me?

Why did you leave me, Mum?
Why am I alone?
Please come back.
I don't want to be alone anymore.

It's not very nice
For a little girl like me.
I'm all alone in this horrible house.
I'm here on my own.
No one else but me.

Please come back, Mum.
I don't like it any more.

I don't like my school anymore, Mum.
No one plays with me.
No one likes me.
I'm all alone.
Please come back, Mum.

Roxanne Orwell (10)
Grove Primary School

Animal Families

My mum is like a dolphin
Because she is cute and beautiful.

My dad is like a giraffe
Because he is tall and he likes to walk.

My brother is like a dragon
Because he likes to fight and he goes red.

My cousin is like a butterfly
Because she always laughs and is bright.

My best friend is like a cat
Because she always plays with me.

Georgia Davis (9)
Grove Primary School

Tropical, Tropical

Tropical, tropical, makes me feel light,
Tropical, tropical, it's a fruity delight.
Melons, oranges, peaches and pears,
Try a smoothie if you dare.

These fruits not only taste yummy,
They are very good for your tummy.
So have five a day
And keep the doctors at bay.

Shriya Chandarana (9)
Grove Primary School

Summer

Summer is coming
So I start humming
The lovely blue sky
Makes me so happy
There's no more reason to cry
The flowers are yellow, orange and red
Come out to play, my friend said
On the holiday weekend of May
I visit the farm
To see the horses munch on the golden hay.

Amber Sawali (8)
Grove Primary School

My Friend Pebbles

She loves her smelly basket
Her old blanket too
She loves to chew up toys
She loves to make a noise
She loves to sleep under a tree
I'm glad she also loves me.

Laura Hayden (9)
Grove Primary School

Grove Primary School

School rules
It's cool
Having fun
Everyone.

School is cool
School is cool
Having fun
For everyone.

The teachers shout
We get sent out
We play football
It's very cool.

School is cool
School is cool
Having fun
For everyone.

I like doing sums
Especially easy ones
Recess rocks
We laugh a lot.

School is cool
School is cool
Having fun
For everyone.

George Simpson (9)
Grove Primary School

Animal Haiku

A sad, hungry dog
Lies waiting behind the door
Waiting for its food.

Chris Matua (9)
Grove Primary School

Football Mad

Monday's football
hear them scream
Tuesday's football
all about the team
Wednesday
you go swimming
Thursday
you come back blinging
Go back to football the next day
thinking we're not going to lose
Then you win
you're on the booze!
Football
a dream for some
Football
a dream for everyone.

Alice Chandler (10)
Grove Primary School

The Dog

My dad
Was glad
To see me
Oh a bee
I got the jar
It didn't go far
We went to the park
I played with Mark
We bought a dog
He ate a log.

Stefan James (9)
Grove Primary School

Everyone In My Family Is An Animal

My mum is like a swan
Because she's always looking after herself
And trying to make herself look pretty.
My dad is like a gorilla
Because he is very tall and he is strong.
My brother is like a rat
Because he is small and can sometimes be nasty.
My uncle David is like a chimpanzee
Because he is always mucking around
And he is very funny.

My cousin Lauren is like a butterfly
Because she is very pretty.
My uncle Barry is like a hippo
Because he is quite large.
My grandma is like a goldfish
Because she loves to swim.
My cousin Marni is like a peacock
Because she is the best cousin in the world.
My nan is like a mother hen
Because she is really kind and I love her.

Kimberley Akaloo (9)
Grove Primary School

Christmas

C hristmas is the day when Jesus was born in Bethlehem.
H appiness and joy will shine in the glory of God.
R eligions pray to their gods.
I fast at Christmas time because of Jesus' birth.
S ymbols help people to come and pray to gods and the saints.
T here is a time to play and a time to pray.
M y memory tells me that there is no other god stronger than God.
A nimals and plants are healthy and grow quickly
S igns always show the way if you are blessed.

Dorian Amoah (10)
Grove Primary School

Lulu?

What have you done wrong now, Lulu?
Was all my mum ever said.
What have you done wrong now, Lulu?
She made me wish I was dead.

Why did you say those things, Mother?
Why did you make me cry?
I said that I was sorry Mother
But I guess you weren't satisfied.

What have you done wrong now, Lulu?
Saying it over and over in my head.
What have you done wrong now, Lulu?
Sending me to bed.

Why did you scream at me, Mother?
Why did you send me to bed?
I didn't like it, Mother
So I ran away instead.

I told you I was fine, Mother
I was round my friend's.
Why did you take me home, Mother?
I didn't like what you said.

What have you done wrong now, Lulu?
She repeated in my head.
What have you done wrong now, Lulu?
Sending me to bed.

Leanne Sands (10)
Grove Primary School

Happiness

Happiness is a new football,
Happiness is 2 hat-tricks in football,
Happiness is meeting new friends,
Happiness is sleeping over your friend's house,
Happiness is a pair of new, shiny trainers.

Ellis Tucker (9)
Grove Primary School

Daydreaming Of Being A Pop Star

I stare and daydream into space,
But suddenly time begins to race.
I dream of being a pop star on stage,
Wearing designer clothes is all the rage.

I am into the stare,
I've got great hair.
Wearing beautiful clothes,
Like pink and two tones.

I am a star,
Don't drive in a car.
I am in a Benz goin' round the block,
I am not boring, I totally rock.

I am now on stage,
I'm gonna sing and dance.
I'm gonna show off to all the lads,
I'm gonna stare and trance.

Reaghan Hearn (10)
Grove Primary School

Friendship

Friendship is like a dream come true.
Friendship is giving each other presents.
Friendship is having an ice cream together.
Friendship is playing together.
Friendship is looking after each other.
Friendship is sharing things together.
Friendship is going on trips together.
Friendship is going shopping together.
Friendship is doing each other's hair.
Friendship is having the same things.

Anisa Jaman (9)
Grove Primary School

When My Friend Comes Along

Hello, my name is Dennis.
I am very good at tennis.
My teacher asked me
'What sports are you good at?'
I say all sports.
But I am very good at cricket.
I went for the wicket
And I hit it.
But my friend got mad
And frustrated when he missed it.
I am good at baseball
Our team always wins the game.
But one thing's for sure
When my friend comes along
We always start all over again.
I am good at football
But I want to be a goalkeeper
But when my friend comes along
I just can't say no
But when he goes in goal
He is a daydreamer.
I am good at golf
And so is my friend
But I think you have heard enough
And now it is
    The end.

Harry Glassgow (10)
Grove Primary School

Happiness

Happiness is a kiss goodnight
Happiness is a friend to talk to
Happiness is a sunny day
Happiness is swimming in cool water
Happiness is a new life forever.

Luke Shepherd (9)
Grove Primary School

Athletics

Pounding, pounding, my heart was pounding
really hard looking down the track
waiting for the gun to go off
hoping that I would win
that wasn't the only thing
on my mind
waiting for someone to
have a false start
would be really
nice for me then
just then the gun went off
I started off really
bright then I just saw
someone shooting
past me. I was going to lose
I was thinking to myself
at least I'm second I
might get a medal.

Luke Roberts (9)
Grove Primary School

Football Forever

Whenever you kick a ball,
you will always feel tall.

When you put on your boots,
you can feel your own roots.

When I score a goal,
I feel like I'm wearing molds.

When you drop your bottle,
you can feel the throttle.

Lee Palmer (10)
Grove Primary School

Daydreaming

Starting to wander into my own land
I picture crowds
lots of football stands.

Looking around I see a sign
and England badge
this can't be right.

Behind me I see a football star
I look in the mirror
it's me, it's me
now I see.

I hear a hoot
I know who I am
I'm the biggest name in football land.

As I come back to Earth
I hear someone calling my name
I stand to bow, I sit down again
as fast as I can.
it's my teacher.

I have to stay in at play
I wander off again
in my own special way.

Holly Trimby (10)
Grove Primary School

Cool Cricket

Basketball
There's none at all
There's only a cricket bat
Who wants to play?
Because you may
One hit of the ball
Then people might say
You're cool.

Arran Sharma (10)
Grove Primary School

To Infinity And Beyond

We're sitting in the rocket
We're about to go
We're discovering a space shuttle
But there's been a big blow.

We can't go into space
We have to stay down here
I wanted to try that food
But I guess I'll have a beer.

I've been told that
The best bit is the sun
Neil Armstrong told me
It's like being shot by a gun.

But hold on there
The rocket is starting to rattle
I think we're going to have blast off
And see that shuttle after all.

Louise Burgess (10)
Grove Primary School

In The Playground

Back in the playground prison
Back in the playground prison
It's where I had to be.
They say they are going to be nice to me
But no, they squash me like a bug
I dig a hole to hide
But they find me inside.
I like my school, but I hate the prison.
It is the worst place
In the world.

Georgia Louise Stone (10)
Grove Primary School

Sport Is Great

I like running,
When you use your legs,
Just like my grandma,
Sticks clothes up with pegs.

Exercise is good for you,
Cos it makes you fit,
Just when you're about,
To go up for a bit.

Sport is good for you,
It is great fun,
When you are doing sports,
Why don't you go get a bun?

Basketball is fun,
But you need a net,
While you're having fun,
Go and get a pet.

Falina Maisuria (9)
Grove Primary School

Nowhere

Nowhere to go,
Nowhere to stay,
Nowhere to enjoy
Nowhere to play.

Nowhere to run,
Nowhere to hide,
Nowhere to get away
From this awful life of mine.

Nowhere to sleep
Nowhere to cry,
Because of this war
No one is nice.

Sean Thomas (10)
Grove Primary School

Friendship

Friendship is playing nicely.
Friendship is playing together.
Friendship is being nice.
Friendship is having a friend.
Friendship is being friendly.
Friendship is playing kindly.
Friendship is like being close.
Friendship is like being a good friend.
Friendship is like having good friends.
Friendship is like being happy with your friends.
Friendship is playing nice games with each other.
Friendship is having a new member of the family.
Friendship is like having a buddy.
Friendship makes you feel good inside.
Friendship makes your heart beat fast.
Friendship is happy for people inside.
Friendship is like having everything you ever wanted in your life.
Friendship is having a good life.
Friendship can go a long way.
Friendship is best for you and your friend.
Friendship is joyful inside.
Friendship is something that makes you feel much happier inside.

Caitlin McDonnell (9)
Grove Primary School

Friendship

Friendship is being kind and being helpful.
Friendship is like a dream.
Friendship is playing nicely.
Friendship is a nice thing.
Friendship is playing 'It'.
Friendship is playing 'Vampires'.

Haris Jabbar (9)
Grove Primary School

Bullying

Please don't bully me
I feel sad and horrid
When you bully me
I feel bad and worried
Please don't shout at me
It makes me feel I want to cry
And to die.

I run away from bullies
I stop and look around me,
All I see is bullies running
All around me.

I do not like bullies
When they stand and stare
They bully me so bad
That they don't even care.

Zahra Khan (10)
Grove Primary School

The Bully

I come out to play,
There is something to say,
Here comes the bully,
Storming with anger,
The trap has happened, I'm shrinking,
The bully stamps the ground.
Shaking, shaking,
It is making me feel like I am an ant,
I scurry along,
He's making me worried.
I live no more
The bully with all its anger.
It stamps on me.
My death has come.

Arun Sharma (9)
Grove Primary School

Happiness

Happiness is a new football.
Happiness is scoring a hat-trick.
Happiness is going to Southend.
Happiness is going to the seaside.
Happiness is going on holiday.
Happiness is meeting new friends.
Happiness is playing games.

Djamel Chaalal (9)
Grove Primary School

Weapons

Guns, guns
They are so powerful
They are so bad
When they shoot across
It kills somebody
Guns are not a toy to play with.

David Sohal (10)
Grove Primary School

Shark Haiku

An aquatic shark
Waiting in the coral reef
Fish swim unaware.

Erin Clover Robinson (9)
Grove Primary School

Skeleton Haiku

Skeleton's bones move,
Like glass bouncing on the floor,
Crash, bang, very loud!

Amy Wood (9)
Grove Primary School

Playground Prison

I hide in places in the playground
Wondering, scared, who will they pick on today?
I want to play, but I'm scared about what they will do or say.
I am sad for the people who get hurt today.
Will they have racist words to say
Or will they kill insects for play?
In the prison-like playground today.

Gerry Oakes (10)
Grove Primary School

Skeleton Haiku

Scary and bony
Mysterious and spooky
The skeleton boy.

Michael Bolton (10)
Grove Primary School

Animal Haiku

Fly-eating lizards
Camouflaged in the branches
Flies land unaware.

Thanusheeyaa Santhiramathirvan (8)
Grove Primary School

Skeleton Haiku

Hard, strong skeleton
Bony bodies are creepy
I do not like them.

Bobby Lomas (9)
Grove Primary School

Midnight Man

The midnight man, he visits me
Every night on Hallowe'en
His fiery eyes warm the night
While his broad branch arms
Hold me tight.
He tucks me in with twig-like fingers
And sings soft lullabies with this soothing voice.
I love the midnight man
And am sad to see him leave
But I know I will see him again.

Cathy Clewley (11)
Hazelmere County Junior School

Angel

You are the angel,
As sweet as the sky,
As soft as the wind, as it floats by.
Round the corner,
Up and down,
Give me a smile, not a frown.
The wings of the ocean,
As a velvet blanket comes away,
The boy, the farmer's son, sleeps in the hay.

Delanie Blastock (10)
Hazelmere County Junior School

Brownies

B rownies are friendly
R ound the toadstool
O ver the world
W e do good turns
N ice to our friends
I n touch with nature
E xploring new things
S isters together, helping each other.

Hannah Underwood (8)
Hazelmere County Junior School

Midnight!

Frankenstein is asleep
Dracula's alarm clock is going beep, beep
Ghosts are waiting under the stairs
Poltergeists throw furniture up in the air
Werewolves are lurking under your bed
Witches stir potions made with frogs' heads
There are monsters and scary things everywhere
So keep your light on and remember
Beware!

Katie Stevens (11)
Hazelmere County Junior School

The Sea

The sea is a rumbling, tumbling leopard cub,
He rolls and rolls so elegantly,
He slices through the rocks with his sharp claws,
He burrows into the soft, thick sand,
He bites the beach with his pointy teeth,
Then home he runs again
Until tomorrow.

Kimberley Davies (11)
Holland Park Primary School

My Two Rabbits

My two rabbits
Are ten weeks old
Jasmine's nervous
But Harvey's quite bold.

Jasmine is black
With a little white belly
She sits on my lap
And watches the telly.

Harvey is blue
Well, a sort of blue/grey
His favourite pastime
Is eating the hay.

Well, I've got to go now
And clean them out
Because if I don't . . .
My mum will shout!

Charley Manners (10)
Holland Park Primary School

Arty Fun

If I could paint a picture
It would be of the countryside
With blue skies and green grass
And animals side by side.

If I could paint a picture
It would be of a bear
With lovely hair
And I will let it have fresh air.

If I could paint a picture
It would be me shooting at goal
With the crowd's humungous roar
With the back of my soul.

James Bettis (10)
Holland Park Primary School

The Travelling Mouse

I've sampled different dishes,
In lots of countries afar,
And the ones that I tell you now,
Are the ones I've eaten so far.

Ponies' tails with dragons' scales,
And a string from Elvis' guitar.
Mouldy cheese with scabs from knees,
And just a pinch of tar.

I've been to France, I took a glance,
It was the place for me,
And I ate frogs' legs and clothes line pegs,
But I had to dash home for tea.

I've been to every place in the world,
As you can plainly see,
But the only thing I've never sampled,
Is a dried up, barbecued pea.

Sam Seago (11)
Holland Park Primary School

My Garden

My garden is full of bright, beautiful colours.
Pinks, purples, reds and greens,
Prickly pushes, majestic trees,
So many flowers, they look like butterflies.

The flapping of the doves,
The chirping of a red robin,
The buzzing of a bee as it sucks pollen,
The scamper of a squirrel as it escapes from a big, black cat.

Oh! how I love my garden.
Somewhere to be quiet,
Somewhere to have fun,
And somewhere to enjoy the evening sun.

Sarah Allerton (10)
Holland Park Primary School

The Greedy Grinch Food Song

I love all kinds of different food
Especially frogs with tea,
Enormous dragons eggs
Come fresh from the sea,
And juicy ants and elephants
Make a lovely recipe!
Scrummy and yummy bat wings,
You surely must agree!

I will eat lava beetle legs
And a scrumptious, slimy slug,
Spiders hairs with the insides of a beautiful bug,
Tasty hedgehogs spikes
With a dash of ants blood in a jug,
To finish it off add a tail
Of a plump pug!

At restaurants I have posh food,
Dumplings with wax, yahoo!
If I am thirsty I will have
Mouldy cows milk, moo!
For main course which is the best part
Is roasted kangaroo,
I don't stay around for dessert
Because I'm full, too da loo!

Olivia Burfoot (10)
Holland Park Primary School

Palm Trees

All you can feel is a warm breeze
Blowing through the palm trees.
As part of the gentle sea breeze
From faraway seas.

Amber Watts (10)
Holland Park Primary School

The Beach

The waves come crashing,
The white foam churning,
The seagulls squawking,
Looking for food.

Propellers rotating,
Sails waving,
And boats sailing along the horizon,
Slowly, as they do.

Children playing,
Making sandcastles,
Swimming in the water,
Oh, how cold!

Pretty seashells to collect,
All different colours, shapes and sizes too,
Plenty of stones washed by the sea,
What a lovely day for you and me.

Georgia Hickey (9)
Holland Park Primary School

Football

Football, oh football,
It is so fun,
Kicking the ball around all day,
Arsenal are number one.

Down the side and cross it in,
The forward ran into the area,
Some player ran down the wing,
Whistle the Arsenal fans continued to sing.

Class players such as Henry,
Are so quick downfield,
Stars in first team carry on rising,
Whilst the youngsters continue to build.

Oliver Will (10)
Holland Park Primary School

The Birdsong

I've eaten many minging things in my time
Rabbit eyes and frogs spawn and drinking lots of grime
I like all the thing especially fried rice
But you really have to try dead mice.

I've eaten sick burgers made by the greatest men alive
And mouldy legs, they taste like a beehive
I don't eat candy because it's dandy
But I definitely eat fruit because it helps you poop.

I often eat logs especially minced dogs
But you must admit I really like my bull hogs
I don't drink much apart from snail slime
Whatever I eat only costs a dime.

I eat juicy rats, they go best with cream
Don't forget cooked mudagies you can find them on the green
I like my grasshoppers squished and squashed and mashed
to a pulp
I gobble them down with one big gulp.

Ian Porter (10)
Holland Park Primary School

My Mum

She is a rocking chair swaying to and fro,
She's an elegant eagle floating through the air,
She is a nocturnal owl asleep through the day,
She's the middle of the day,
A tulip growing through the day,
A spicy prawn cocktail that every boy likes,
The hooting of an owl,
A god trying to help,
    That's my mum!

Christopher Gadeke (10)
Holland Park Primary School

The Strange Food Eater

I've eaten many weird and tasty dishes in my life,
Even though I haven't even got a lovely wife.
I get very sad because I am all alone,
Because I have no contact at all because I ate the phone.

The food I like the most is slugs with hairs all over,
I've even tried to eat a four-leafed clover.
I really like chicken with bugs inside,
Mixed with sloppy custard, they really do slide.

Tomorrow for dinner I will have dog tails,
Nicely on the side with big, fat snails.
Then for pudding I shall have a big mushroom cake,
But I haven't got the money for goodness sake!

For tea I will have biscuit worms, they have a lovely smell,
They will go down my belly like a big, long well.

Chris Wilson (11)
Holland Park Primary School

The Bear's Song

I've eaten many crazy and delicious dishes in my time
Like mashed rats with a slice of picked grime
And eyes and spice - they're really nice
When barbecued in their prime.

I've eaten live bug burgers by the worst cooks there are
And boiled cats and green bugs eggs and bees stewed in tar
And snails in pails and earwig tails
And cattle by the jar.

I often eat boiled cricket,
They're grand when served beside minced dung beetle and
        curried snail
And have you ever tried bed bug toes and shellfish roes
Most delicately baked?

Eddie Parsons (11)
Holland Park Primary School

The Hababubalicious Poem

I've gobbled many gross and gorgeous dishes in my time,
Like grilled flies and scrambled eyes and snails served with limes,
With rats and cats served on mats, all roasted in their grime,
But always be very sure to eat up all the slime.

I've munched fresh frogs and lovely hogs, that frequently taste nice,
With sausage pots and tadpole logs all eaten with crab rice,
And minced hippos with silver loaves, improved with juicy lice,
I sure do like my scrumptious meals when they are nicely diced.

I crave the taste of sour boar when they are all mushed up,
With lots of tasty tentacles, mixed round on a cup.
A plate of lizards legs that come with lovely churned up pup,
So make sure that you eat your tea and gobble this lot up.

Finally I'd like to say how yummy these meals are,
They're the best that I have ever tasted in the world by far.
My favourite is a hairy horse that comes with scrumptious tar,
I hope you like these things as well, although they are bizarre.

Hannah Baker (11)
Holland Park Primary School

The Ooey Gooey Song

I've eaten many weird and gorgeous dishes in my time,
Like jellied snakes and orange cakes,
And beetles dipped in slime,
And rats and bats to fill the cats,
When cooked in their own prime
(But don't forget to sprinkle them
With lovely gooey grime.)

I've eaten crunchy fingers by the worst cooks there are,
And munched up frogs and diced up dogs
And prawn tails dipped in tar,
And segs of pegs and earwigs legs,
And woodlice under the jar.
(A woodlice could be let out with a splash of vinegar.)

Kelly Holdbrook (11)
Holland Park Primary School

The Fuddle-Doop's Song

I've eaten many different and strange dishes in my time,
Like spiders' legs and chicken eggs that's in a shop called Chime,
And they sell some yucky icky lime,
And lice with some ice is at an expensive price,
Especially with some grime.
I often eat boiled snake with bat wings from my jar of cakes,
And hairy nits on a stick that smell a bit,
Take a few minutes to bake.
(Which can be improved by a bit of chocolate shake.)

I'm crazy for spaghetti made of wiggly worms for lunch,
And on the side fried cricket wings are my very favourite munch,
I really love the sound of those loud cricket wings go -
                                 crunch, crunch, crunch,
When I'm eating in a hunch.

I've tried many strange and different dishes in my time,
Slimy and crunchy and full of nice munchies,
But I must say that my favourite is
My mum's lime apple and ant pie with a hint of slime,
Even though afterwards it's itchy inside for a little time.

Faye Walton (11)
Holland Park Primary School

Cats And Kittens!

When I see a cat I can't help but want to pick it up,
When I touch a cat I often want to take it home.
When I see a cat I always feel so delighted,
When I hear the purr I don't want to put it down.

When I see a kitten my heart glows with pleasure,
When I touch a kitten I think how soft it is.
When I see a kitten I have a constant yearning of happiness,
When I hear a kitten's squeak my heart melts.

Clare Gravatt (10)
Holland Park Primary School

The Weeblogger's Song

My life has come across some very odd and mad delights,
Like blogger snails, chestnut tails and stewed giant termites,
And I once ate some chillied crates
That kept me up all night,
(The wooden part burnt my heart and gave me quite a fright!)

When I swallow feathers they tickle in my throat,
So then I find a castle and guzzle all its moat.
My very favourite starter
Is usually on toast,
(Sometimes it is living but normally a ghost!)

I like a swig of engine oil, paraffin and turps,
When I drink it quick enough it gives me chronic burps.
A naked flame around me really doesn't work,
(One big burp, one big bang, it really does quite hurt!)

Trifle jelly, ice cream, they're really not my taste,
When they're put in front of me I really do make haste.
Please do give me termites, wriggling in some nuclear waste,
(Mix it up with dynamite to make a lovely paste!)

Sam Mahoney (11)
Holland Park Primary School

The Spider!

The hunter hanging from his web,
Caught a fly and then he said,
'This looks like a tasty treat,
I think I'll eat this delicious meat.'

'Oh, please don't eat me, hairy beast,
I'm too small to make a feast.'
But to this plea he did not listen,
He ate the fly till his fangs did glisten.

Harry Ryan (10)
Holland Park Primary School

Fireworks

The fireworks swirl and twirl in the air
Everyone looks and stares
Everyone waits . . . until . . . the . . . right . . . moment . . . then . . .
Crackle! Pop! Bang!
Everyone cheers, claps, whistles but wait . . .
More comes
Sizzle! Bang! Boom!
More claps, more applause and more cheering comes.
But then the grand finale comes
Boom! Bang! Crackle!
Pop! Boom! Sizzle! Boom! Bang!
More and more applause and cheering
And whistling flies through the air.
After the cheering stops it all goes silent
And soon we go home.

Kyle Lowis (10)
Holland Park Primary School

May The 22nd

May the 22nd, my birthday,
I've just woken up at 6 o'clock in the morning,
I've run into Mum and Dad's room to get my presents.
Dan drove me round my gran's house
And I got my presents from them too.
I'm going to the leisure centre and I'm playing football,
I hope it doesn't rain on May the 22nd!
I'm having a party at the Eastcliff
I will play from 2.00 till 4.00,
Then I'll have McDonald's with my friends,
They'll all sing Happy Birthday
And then we'll have cake!
I like May the 22nd
I'm sure it will be great!

Liam Torr-Clark (10)
Holland Park Primary School

A Winter's Day

Frilly yellow catkins,
Hanging on a tree,
Lovely bright sun,
What a sight to see!

Clouds like cotton wool,
Snow as soft as a teddy,
Hands hurt a lot,
For bed, I am ready!

Freezing cold body,
Very, very numb,
Feels like candyfloss,
I hope more showers come.

Sparkly snow,
Feels like flour for a cake,
Frosty snowmen,
Come on, let's celebrate!

Hannah Needham (9)
Holland Park Primary School

Running

R eady on the starting blocks
U mpire holding the gun aloft
N erves jangling
N o time for thoughts
I   n the end
N obody loses
G old for everyone!

That's the fun of running.

Matthew Cross (10)
Holland Park Primary School

Mother Parrot's Advice

Carefully wash your feathers
To get out all the bugs
Be kind to all your family
And give them lots of hugs.

Never fly fast
Or you will crash
Wherever you are going
You will be there in a flash.

Eat lots of leaves
So you will get strong
If you fly very fast
You will land in Hong Kong.

Sit sensibly in a tree
Or you could easily fall
Always look after your plumage
And a stunning mate will call.

Thomas Moodey (8)
Holland Park Primary School

My Dolphin

Water diver,
Like the wind,
Blue sparkle,
Crescent shape,
Smooth skin,
Silent sound,
Circle swimmer,
Also friendly with a smile.

Laura Vile (9)
Holland Park Primary School

Mother's Advice

Always eat up all your vegetables
Or you'll never grow to be strong
And if you don't do your homework
That would be quite wrong.

Always brush your teeth twice a day
Or your teeth may rot
Hold on to the horse tight
Then there's a chance for it to trot.

Always put your seatbelt on
Or you could end up in a crash
Don't open the door when driving
Or you'll go flying in the trash.

Never tell a lie
Because you'll always get found out
Always do what mum says
Or she'll give you a shout.

Daniel Fairbanks (8)
Holland Park Primary School

Showstopper

S uspenseful.
H ow can you not like it?
O verwhelming fun.
W hen you read it, you cannot stop!
S urprisingly an action-filled adventure.
T op marks.
O ver the top on Victorian-style life.
P eople will like it.
P ersonally I thought it was superb!
E veryone can enjoy it.
R eminds me of Montmorency.

Thomas Wilkinson (10)
Holland Park Primary School

Sweet Pea Fairies

Here are the sweetest colours
Fragrance very sweet
Here are silky pods of peas
Not for us to eat!

Here's a fairy's sister,
Trying on with care,
Such a grand new bonnet,
For the baby there.

Does it suit you, baby?
Yes, I really think
Nothing's more becoming
Than this pretty pink!

Kirsty Muir (10)
Holland Park Primary School

Ingredients!

Take a bit of noise,
Some smelly things as well,
Mix them all up thoroughly,
Get a devil from Hell,
Take a bit of biting,
A pinch of pinching too,
Cook for ten minutes,
Sprinkle on a telling off from Mother,
And there you have it,
My little brother!

Ava Pickett (10)
Holland Park Primary School

The Simpsons

The Simpsons are the freaks, up the neighbourhood.
They walk about, an odd group, look out, you really should.

Maggie's small, quiet and sweet, she loves to sit and cry,
Sucking on her dummy, whilst she stands and waves goodbye.

Lisa's smart, brave and bold, she likes to run around,
Winding up her brother, whilst her father makes rude sounds.

Bart's leary, loud and trouble, he likes to be so funny,
Wreaking lots of havoc, 'cause he wants his father's money.

Marge is wise, clever and neat, she loves to do her hair,
Moaning at the children, as she watches in despair.

Homer's fat, plump and thick, he sits and rubs his tum,
Drinking duff with beer, as he chews and sucks his thumb.

The Simpsons are a big, weird bunch, who don't get on all days,
Arguing forever, as they go their separate ways.

Luke Elkes (10)
Holland Park Primary School

The Wonders Of The Sun

The wonders of the sun,
Can fill you with fun,
Playing with my brother hand in hand,
It can fill you with glee as you splash in the sea,
And it warms every grain of the sand,
It makes living things grow,
And it melts away snow,
Making rainbow puddles appear,
There's a smile on my face as the moon takes its place,
As I dream of my day on the pier.

Jonah Lees (8)
Holland Park Primary School

The Fatopillar's Song

I've been to many places and tasted such strange things,
Like slimy rats and roasted gnats and jellied bats' wings,
But best of all I have to say I like the grimy stings,
Of scorpions and killer bees and even toads that sing.

I've eaten bones and sticks and Weetabix and surely you'll agree,
Dung cake mix and horses spit are extremely yummy,
But what's really, really nice is a hairy lion's knee,
But don't forget to dip it in the sap of a tree.

I like puss-filled slugs and curried bugs and have you ever tried
The nose of a grizzly bear most delicately fried?
A nice, fat, juicy bug from the cave where I reside,
Sadly this dish disagrees with my insides.

Now comes most unfortunately the end of my speech,
I may have much more to say but I don't want to preach.
Many of these dishes are almost out of reach,
But definitely not the Australian leech.

Louise Rodwell (11)
Holland Park Primary School

Football Crazy

When the players go on the pitch,
Surprisingly they've got a stitch.
When they score a goal,
Best of all cheers Roald Dahl.
When the referee shows the red card,
I feel all hard.
When the ball goes paste the goalie,
The team does a roly poly.
Football is the best,
Better than the rest.

Louis Lavallin (10)
Holland Park Primary School

The Silent Sea

Winter has passed
No stormy nights,
Spring has sprung
Now off to the beach.

The waters are still
Like a sleeping hound,
Sandcastles are built
Ice creams melt on the ground.

Children laugh and scream
As they romp in the sea,
Mums sit admiring
The beautiful view.

The sea still lies
Not making a sound,
Not daring to awake
The sleeping hound.

Lydia Hills (10)
Holland Park Primary School

A Winter's Day

Snow is cold,
Snow makes you freeze,
Snow is very fluffy,
Snow makes you sneeze.

Snow is like a teddy,
Snow is very bright,
Snow is as soft as a lamb's tail,
Snow is pure white.

Snow stings your hand,
Snow wafts in the breeze,
Snow is very crunchy,
Snow freezes your knees.

Megan Ganderton (9)
Holland Park Primary School

My Mummy!

My mummy
Is very caring
She loves me too
She's very good at sharing.

My mummy
Is very nice
She helps me with everything
She cuddles me very kindly.

My mummy
Is always happy
She never wears a frown
And when I was a baby she changed my nappy.

My mummy
Runs me to school
She's always fun
She is really cool.

I couldn't be happier and luckier!

Bethany (8)
Holland Park Primary School

Snow

Snow is crunchy
Snow is cold
Snow is soft like a teddy bear
Snow makes you bold.

Snow is fun
Snow makes my fingers sting
Snow is like a white carpet
Snow does winter bring.

Francesca Dulieu (8)
Holland Park Primary School

Terezin Concentration Camp

I have dreamt in my wildest dreams,
To get out of this horrid dump,
To get back to the food and fresh air,
Go back to the laughter and fun.

But dreams are just dreams,
And soon I'll have none,
No food or fresh air,
No laughter or fun.

I'm afraid I'll die,
By a German's ghastly gun,
And then all will be over,
No laughter or fun.

I wish it was over,
I wish I could run,
Get away from this place,
To the laughter and fun.

People weeping, people shouting,
People swearing at the sun,
Suffering from typhus and flu,
Of course, no laughter or fun.

Stefanie Klarner (11)
Holland Park Primary School

Snow

S now is cold and crunchy
N icely perched on bare branches
O ne big, glistening carpet
W hite as a barn owl in the morning sleet.

Courtney Eastman (9)
Holland Park Primary School

War's No Joke, War's No Fun

The siren wails,
You freeze and run,
War's no joke,
War's no fun.

You crouch in the shelter,
Planes overhead,
You hear an explosion,
You know someone's dead.

You take a peek,
Afraid of what you might find,
You see someone's pale face,
Knowing their death was quick and unkind.

The siren wails,
You freeze and run,
War's no joke,
War's no fun.

Adam Gardiner (11)
Holland Park Primary School

The Angry Sea

The sea is a horse,
Rampaging across the land,
Wandering everywhere.

The sea is a lion,
Untamed, roaring in his lair,
Ferociously lashing at the cliffs.

The sea is a tiger,
Fighting at night,
Bashing and clashing, showing his might.

The sea is a monkey,
Jumping around,
Leaping and bounding over the rocks.

James Smart (11)
Holland Park Primary School

The Mad Sea

Gigantic waves,
crashing in the sea.
Sea creatures dashing,
quickly as can be.
Starfish grabbing,
onto huge rocks.
Barnacles sticking,
to anything they can.
Dark grey clouds,
hovering in the sky.
Crabs digging under the sand,
before they get caught.
Necklace shells scattering,
searching for their prey.
Limpets sucking,
so tightly to the rocks.
Danger could be anywhere!

Natalie Creelman (11)
Holland Park Primary School

Send A Smile

S miles cost nothing.
E verybody has a smile.
N ever frown.
D on't cry.

A lways smile.

S end a smile.
M eet new friends.
I f someone is feeling down, throw away their frown.
L eave a smile on someone's face.
E veryone deserves to be happy.
  So smile!

Gemma Day
Holland Park Primary School

Evacuees

As I went to line up
I wondered who could pick me
Before I meet the family
I wondered if I would see my mum again.

As I got picked
I wondered if I would like them
As I looked at them
I wondered if I would see my mum again.

When I got to their home
I wondered if they had a cat
As I unpacked
I wondered if I would see my mum again.

As I went to bed
I wondered what I would dream about
In my dream
I saw my mum again.

Emily Gallone (10)
Holland Park Primary School

The Seaside

As my feet touch the soft sand,
I feel burning all over the land.

The scorching sun shines on my face,
As I walk along the beach at a steady pace.

I stare out to sea,
Which I'm sure stares back at me.

The sea glistens from the gleaming sun,
As I paddle in the water with my loving mum.

I can hear all the seagulls squawking,
As I carry on walking.

The sun sets and the beach is silent.

Claire Hills (10)
Holland Park Primary School

The Caveman's Song

I've come across some weird and super servings in my time,
Like mammoth noses and giant roses dunked in chalky grime,
With chillied hogs and fat roast dogs
When stamped to a slime
But you mustn't forget a bowl with a large, pickled lime.

I've eaten juicy parasites and log with termites in,
With fresh beeswax and raincoats and deer pierced with a pin,
And centipede head with tadpole spread,
Plus monkfish by the tin.
Just remember to add a pinch of powdered mammoth chin.

Another favourite meal of mine that I really love to chew
Is curried rats and smoked worm cats baked in goat fondue.
They're really nice mixed with head lice,
And put in gizzard stew.
It may taste rough but with enough you'll trot off to the loo.

I've always loved to chew and tear the udders of a cow,
And also crunch the heads off kittens when they say meow
Or suck the brains with hollow veins
From the hind legs of a sow.
(But to get the vein you'll go insane and drink your granny's chow.)

Robert McNair Wilson (11)
Holland Park Primary School

My Apple Poem

My apple is as fresh as a new melon,
Inside my apple looks as crunchy as a freshly burnt chip,
My apple is as juicy as a brand new watermelon,
My apple feels as smooth as a laminated piece of paper,
The stem feels as rough as an edge of a piece of wood,
My apple smells as fresh as a new piece of French bread.

Jonathan Strutt (11)
Holland Park Primary School

The Strangest Of Dinners

I've eaten many different and delicious things in my time,
Slugs and bugs covered in lots of gooey grime.
Cockroaches taste better with a hint of lime,
But don't forget to add a bit of saucy slime.

I've eaten many other things such as lovely crusty snails,
But the funniest thing I've ever eaten is lizards with golden tails.
The one thing I must comment on is jelly with rusty nails,
But never, ever eat it with silver fishes scales.

I crave for the taste of a hairy frog,
Beetle bugs on a spotted log.
Every dog always tastes better with a hint of fresh heather,
These make a tasty bite as light as a feather.

For my Christmas dinner
This is a certain winner,
Large worms that are flatter,
All served on a golden platter.

Laura Gilbert (11)
Holland Park Primary School

My Nectarine

My nectarine is as bright as when the sun goes down,
My nectarine is as smooth as polished wood,
Inside my nectarine it is as a rough as a stormy sea,
My nectarine smells like a brand new day,
My nectarine tastes like eating goodness,
My nectarine is the best.

Georgina Woolfe (11)
Holland Park Primary School

Auschwitz

I saw the stained blood
On the ground,
As people stuttered and stared
All around.

It was the darkest place
I had ever seen,
Worse than my worst nightmare,
Very obscene.

Fleshless bodies,
Only skin and bone,
Shaved heads,
Horrible tattooed numbers,
Scarred for life.

It finally happened,
It was my turn to starve,
I wanted to get out,
I wanted to be
Free!

William Anderson-White (11)
Holland Park Primary School

My Fruit Salad

A recipe for my fruit salad:

Cut into soft, sludgy slices,
Add two crunchy, juicy apples,
Take a mouth-watering, sweet melon,
Slice all the succulent flesh,
Take sour, bright redcurrants,
Chop juicy strawberries,
Put in chunks of moist nectarines,
Now add water with sweet sugar,
Stir gently.
Now you have a perfect fruit salad.

Aaron Redpath (11)
Holland Park Primary School

Pets

I've got a pet
And I took it to the vet
It lives in a hat
It is a cat.

I've got a pet
And I took it to the vet
It stands on a log
It is a dog.

I've got a pet
And I took it to the vet
It made a wish
It is a fish.

I've got a pet
And I took it to the vet
It doesn't like to swim in the lake
It is a snake.

Lauren Heron (7)
Holly Trees Primary School

Jasper

I have a dog called Jasper,
He's black and white.
If it thunders in the night,
It will give him such a fright.

I have a dog called Jasper,
He's black and white and brown.
If he wakes my mum up,
She'll give him quite a frown.

I have a dog called Jasper,
He's brown and white and black.
If someone ever took him,
I would really want him back.

Emilie Cobb (9)
Holly Trees Primary School

A Summer In A Wood

A wood in summer, bathed in a mellow light,
A breeze, bitter and fresh as a splash of lemon,
Carries sugary-sweet birdsong through the trees,
With a speeding glimmer of a dragonfly,
Dancing over a lake,
And when a sweltering sun,
Contrasts with a refreshing breeze,
It creates a natural and wild duet,
Untouched by man's treacherous hand,
The very air is tranquil and undisturbed,
A shower as soft as a feather,
Blades of grass, emerald-green needles,
Swimming in the murmuring wind,
With the feel of nature's gaze,
The chant of its unique song,
A wood in summer, at day's end,
Mellow light turns to glow,
As clouds, as misty patterns prepare their morn dew,
And when the sun fades out, nothing is lost,
As a summer wood's beauty never dies.

Sophie Drew (11)
Holly Trees Primary School

Animals

A lligator, alligator swimming in the everglades looking for its tea
N ewts swim around day and night chilling in the moonlight
I guanas lying in the dry sand waiting for a fly to come along
M onkeys swinging in the trees with the birds and the bees chasing
the chimpanzees
A nts crawling all around watching out for humans to avoid being
stamped upon
L ions lazing about waiting for a zebra to pass
S nakes slithering through the grass passing all the animals.

Lauren Gregory & Megan Tuck (10)
Holly Trees Primary School

Esmeralda

Esmeralda is a witch's cat but found it none too easy.
Looping loops and swooping swoops, it made her feel quite queasy.
One wild night by the pale moonlight, she was green with
                                            travel sickness.
She lost her grip and began to slip and found herself broomstickless.
Where she fell, I can't tell, but that's a different story.
After that, the cat went splat, then she felt quite poorly.

When she woke up, she spoke up, 'Wow, that really hurt,
I wish I'd stayed on the broomstick and not fell in the dirt!'
With some regret she went to the vet feeling very bruised.
The vet said she's fine but stay off the wine, but Esmeralda refused.
She decided then to never again, go up in the air and fly.
To stay on the ground where it's safe and sound and keep away
                                            from the sky!

Sarah Anne Brialey (9)
Holly Trees Primary School

The Golden Stallion

Mane lifted high by the raging storm,
Free and wild, a demand of gold,
Horse against the sky, a rear so proud,
Blurred by a storm cloud of stinging-steel rain.
Golden horse, stepping high,
Free and wild, melting into the sky,
Silver flowing mane, cascade of foam,
Let wild by man, free to roam,
Through the forest, galloping, leaving a trail of gold,
Galloping proud, fearless and bold,
Hooves shattering silence with their clashing sound,
Communicating without words, with the passive ground.

Danielle Carr (11)
Holly Trees Primary School

All My Pets

I've got . . .

A hamster and a gerbil
And a fish that goes gurgle.

A dog and a cat
And a long-tailed rat.

A budgie and a bunny
And a mouse that's very funny.

A snail and a snake
And a terrapin called Jake.

My mum says that's enough
I can't have any more
Cos they're doing too much business
On the carpet and the floor!

Amy Simmonds (8)
Holly Trees Primary School

Life

Is life love and hate?
Is it death?
Is it all the sweet things in life?
Is it the flavour and scent of achievement
That carries us through life?
Is it our future and past that makes us who we are?
Is it the caress of love from others that beckon us on?
Is it the secrets we need to make us mellifluously flow?
Is it who we are that makes us what we are?
Is it the time sifting through our fingers?
Is it the ingredients we need to unlock?
Oh yes it is.

Jake Wallace (11)
Holly Trees Primary School

My Friends

I can tell a secret
We can play a game
And we will share a song
Those are my friends.
When I'm down
They're always there
Helping me
Through every tear
Those are my friends.
It doesn't matter
Where I am
But it is better
When they are there because
Those are my friends.
Friends like mine
Are always kind
If they ever left
My heart would cry
To see my friends
Go away
And I would put a tear
In the ocean
And when they found it
I would stop missing them because
Those are my friends
And that's how it would be.
When I fall
And when I call
For those caring, daring, yet great
Friends of mine.

Suelen Tenn (8)
Holly Trees Primary School

Fight For Death

The darkest hour,
A chill in the wind,
A looming shape ahead.
The blanket of night,
The rain of winter.

A guardian of hundreds,
Entrusted with lives.
People swarming around me like ants,
Their faces blank,
Through fear beats through every heart.

A clinking and rustling,
A whispered battle chant.
The battering-ram is ready.
The door screams and shouts,
But now it has fallen.

Scattering like birds,
Women and children retreat.
Crashes and cries,
Deaths by the hundreds,
Deaths by the thousands.

We fight for our country,
And that's how we die.
This is what prides me,
As I rise from my death,
Away from a world of disaster.

Bernadette Rees (11)
Holy Trinity CE Primary School

Battle

Pitch-black, misty night,
Castle hunched like a black cape.
Arrows appearing through the eyes,
Waiting to launch.
Soldiers gathering like a herd of elephants,
Metre long cannons waiting to burst with cannonballs
Directed right at us,
Angry.
Battering-ram bursting with energy,
As we burst through the door,
People scattering like disturbed ants,
The battle has begun.
Screams and shouts bang through our ears,
Arrows raining down on us,
Stopped.
Red blood runs down their faces,
A red cover covers me.

Natalie Fisher (11)
Holy Trinity CE Primary School

The Castle

It was an inky-black night
The weather was still
The army, charging through the trees
Scattered all over the place like a swarm of bees
Bang! A battering-ram smashing the door down
Scalding tar pouring down from the battlements
Burning through their skin
Flying arrows charging through the air
People getting killed
The army has gone away
People lying on the floor, dead
But people have been hiding
Still alive, all lonely.

Jordan Brown (10)
Holy Trinity CE Primary School

To The Start And Finish

As we walk,
Clashing,
Our armour banging,
Like a heart beating.

As if we are threading some thread through a thin loophole,
The strong door guards the castle,
Rushing,
Scattering,
Shaking,
And we're in!

The people scattering like ants,
Running from us,
Tiny,
Frightened.
Have we won or not?

As the night draws on,
Thunder clashes loudly,
As rain pours down,
Dripping,
Cold.
Lightning lights the sky,
Damp,
Now standing face to face with a narrow and lonely gatehouse.

The scary faces stare,
The castle as tall as tree trunks,
The night is as black as a bat,
As tall as a giant.

As we stand like tigers,
Ready to pounce for our prey,
The castle, like a cat stalking,
Sly and discreet,
Camouflaged,
Ready to go.

Melissa Godfrey (10)
Holy Trinity CE Primary School

The Battle

It's a cold, misty night,
We're cramped together,
Trying to keep warm,
But we can't.

Then upon us,
Like a giant,
The castle awaits,
As it is scared to be attacked.

But now I'm strong,
We're like a swarm of wasps,
Ready with their stings to attack,
We're going to be victorious.

Suddenly, as we try to break down the door,
Hot, boiling tar comes down,
The arrows are like the venom from a snake,
But we keep on fighting.

There's screams and shouts,
It's loud with fear,
The clanking of armour,
And thumping of feet.

Swords slashing,
People falling to the ground,
Feeling cold, they flee to their keep,
The battle on the floor is won.

As the keep doors explode,
We kill everyone in our path,
We have defeated them,
We have won the battle.

Elizabeth Barron (11)
Holy Trinity CE Primary School

Attack

The sky covered like a blanket of darkness.
Cold like a tunnel of ice.
Wet like a river.

The castle towering above,
Strong as a tree,
Untouched, undisturbed.

Our armour shattering the castle,
Quiet like a mouse.
Our faces scared but fierce
With camouflaged bodies
We begin!
Our faces scared and frightened.

The battering-ram bashing the doors.
'Help, help!' cry the doors
As we blast through
With arrows stuck in our armour.
Cries and yells come as we slaughter the families.
The war has started.

'Clank, clink!' shout our swords
As we finally conquer the castle.

Daniel Morris (10)
Holy Trinity CE Primary School

The Castle

A black, murky night,
Thick clouds gather above our heads,
Thunder and lightning destroying the sky,
Start to feel cold raindrops like ice cubes
Landing on my face.

The front of the castle is an angry, fierce face
Watching our every move,
Protected by a wall of anger,
Any minute now they will be attacking.

Men gathering like a swarm of bees,
Armour clashing and clanging,
Thousands of mean, angry faces,
Just ready to attack.

Bang! Bang! A battering-ram pelting itself at the door.
The door will just fall into pieces soon.
Crack! The door was forced to the ground.

Shouting and screaming as we run to attack.
Swords and shields hitting men.
Arrows travelling faster than the speed of light
Constantly firing out of the loopholes.
Finally they flee for their lives.

Alex McKenzie (11)
Holy Trinity CE Primary School

Victory Is Ours

A dark, rainy night,
Lightning flies through the sooty sky,
Whining like an injured dog trapped.

The scruffy castle sitting firm,
Loose rocks crumble,
Loopholes, dark and angry like an owl's unblinking eyes.

Shadowed creatures scurrying around,
Stomping and marching in enormous lines,
Walking slowly to the creaky door.

Snatching the battering-ram,
Charging into the wooden door,
Running in as they start to fight.

Clashing swords,
As the opponent's last soldier fell to the muddy floor,
Victory is ours!

Amber Callaghan (10)
Holy Trinity CE Primary School

The Castle

A black night, misty and rain with fog around.
Rain pouring down like buckets of fear.

The castle looks like a sad face staring down upon us
And the castle protected by a wall of sadness.

We are the intruders on this land,
Wanting its jewels.

The battering-ram charging at the door
Like a fierce bull that has been tormented.
The battering-ram weighing us all down.

Eventually we break through, the door crying to us.
The door falling down like a tower of bricks.

As we step through the door, there they are, staring at us.
Blood is shed, harsh fighting upon us.

Luke Gosney (11)
Holy Trinity CE Primary School

The Battle

As the night draws on,
Thunder crashes,
Bang,
The rain storms down,
As we enter the castle bridge,
The towering stones glaring down at us,
The gigantic shield of protection,
The rain bangs down on the army,
Stampeding into the portcullis like elephants galloping,
Out of the loopholes arrows come flying down like a strike
of lightning,

The doors explode open,
We're in,
Screaming, shouting they run,
Nervous as the prey to be caught,
Only one side can win.
Who?

Lauren Britton (10)
Holy Trinity CE Primary School

The Castle

The weather was stormy,
With the thunder crashing,
The castle, a big giant like 'The Hulk'.
The castle like big giant feet.

We are like Concorde racing to the gate.
We are like a torpedo, like a tiger.
The big, heavy, battering-ram slowly crashing towards the door.

The bolt coming straight off.
Soldiers run from us.
Cannons explode.
Guns fire across the walls.
The army defeated!

We're the winner!

Christopher King (11)
Holy Trinity CE Primary School

Castle

A damp, soggy night,
A bolt of lightning striking against our shields,
The floor vibration with the sound of thunder,
Dark, like a pile of soot swarming forwards.

A huge, rock-solid tower,
Like a person clumping his hands around,
Never going to let go,
Eyes appearing through the loopholes.

A black beetle with his armour-plated back,
Shhh!
No noise, a silent beetle quietly moving toe by toe,
Just a silent clash.

Slashing forwards,
Chief giving commands,
The noise dying down,
People surrendering to the floor,
One last breath, we're all *dead!*

Natasha Lamont (11)
Holy Trinity CE Primary School

The Battle

Pitch-black, raining, gloomy, thunder and lightning.
The castle like a Hallowe'en mask, scary and big.
They came from the tree, swarming like bees,
Charging like a tiger roaring.
They're at the door.
They use a battering-ram to try to get in.
We get the hot oil and pour it over them.
They get through, swords everywhere.
People dying all around me.
Blood spilt everywhere.
We have won the battle.

Lee Moffat (11)
Holy Trinity CE Primary School

The Castle

Crack!
A bolt of lightning strikes against us.
Thunder crashes like a giant's enormous foot against the ground.
It's deep black like an angry crow catching its prey.
Looking up at a ginormous tower like a stretching giraffe.
Its scary face and heavy arms coming towards us,
Its rocky walls like razor-sharp teeth.
Deep cuts bleed as I scramble up the wall.
We march towards the castle like a pack of brave, angry wolves.
Our armour clangs as we trudge along.
We are quiet.
Bang!
It's our first charge and attack with the battering-ram.
'Forward!' calls the chief again as we attack.
Whoosh!
The doors wing open, we're in.
Shooting arrows approach us through their loopholes.
We conquer through like someone pushing in a line.
Bang!
No more sound, we have won.
The victory is ours!

Lucy Phillips (10)
Holy Trinity CE Primary School

The Castle

Pitch-black like a bat's wing, sweeping through the sky.
The soggy, wet, dark land. God is against us.
The giant castle wearing a protective coat
To stop us getting in.
As we use our battering-ram to help us to get in.
As the invisible army attacking us from nowhere.
As we try to attack back we are failing to hit
Barely anyone is left.
We have won. Victory is ours.
We have some new land.

Shaun Warren (11)
Holy Trinity CE Primary School

The Battle

Stormy, thundering, furious weather
Clashing sounds from falling objects
Rain dripping off us all
The stony face looking fierce
Looking down into the moat, telling *beware!*
Brick by brick the wall stands straight
Shoulder by shoulder like bunched-up leaves
Ready to charge glaring faces
Not a wink
Flying swarm of wasps
As we try to batter down the door
Yells of burning skins
We're in
Screams from children and women
Blood and men going everywhere like lost sheep.

Have we won the battle?

Lindsey Marsh (11)
Holy Trinity CE Primary School

Success

It was a dark, jet-black night,
Can only see the hot flames flickering.
Marching fiercely at the castle,
Looking like a gruesome giant staring down at us.
Rampaging their territory.
Maybe they don't know we're here.

The army, camouflaged and forcing its way up the hill,
Like a swarm of bees.
Our army going in all directions at the castle,
Finally hitting the front gate with so much force
Using a battering-ram,
Knocking the oak door down,
Raging through, starting a battle,
Staying in our formations as we take on the opposing army.
At the end of the battle success is with us.

David Weir (11)
Holy Trinity CE Primary School

The Castle

I enter the grounds,
The sooty sky patched with fog,
As black as ink,
Just a faint light showing us the way.

The castle, like a giant,
Is towering over me.
Deep in the shadow,
As tough as a bone.

We are a torpedo,
Like a herd of elephants in a bad mood,
Not afraid of anything.

The big, heavy battering-ram slides slowly towards the door,
Boiling hot tar surrounding me.
The door creaks before we finally break in with a clash.

The opposition army are ready,
The clash-clash of swords.
In the gates, people firing at the speed of light
Fortunately missing.
They retreat as 10 brave soldiers step up and win us the battle.

Robert Scott (10)
Holy Trinity CE Primary School

The Castle

Pitch-black like a bat's wing, sweeping through the sky.
The soggy, wet, dark land, God is against us.
The giant castle wearing a protective coat to stop us getting in,
As we use our battering-ram to help us to get in,
As the invisible army attacking us from nowhere,
As we try to attack back.
We are failing to hit and barely anyone is left.
We have won, victory ours, we have some new land.

Bradley Mason (11)
Holy Trinity CE Primary School

The Castle War

Dark shadows forming,
The sun is at its highest,
As bright as a newly-fitted light bulb,
The blue sky as its surroundings.

The castle standing alone,
Like a prison with an eerie smell,
Good things are enclosed,
You just wait!

Metal armour clashing,
Like hungry lion's teeth,
Fierce faces like a tiger,
Marching row by row.

Slashing the ropes of the portcullis,
Making it zoom up like a rocket,
Thud, thud,
The heavy battering-ram charging at the door.

War shouts flooding in our ears,
Like the ocean flooding in,
Clashing of sharp swords,
Arrows like shooting stars.

Soldiers are crying out in despair,
Whimpering like babies,
Retreating to the keep,
The battle has been won!

Hannah Suttling (11)
Holy Trinity CE Primary School

The Castle

Rain lashing from the jet-black sky,
Thunder crashing, lightning flashing,
Roads are flooding,
The wind is howling.

The old, creepy castle standing still,
Wearing away like a snake shedding its skin,
Lopsided,
Scruffy and uncared for,
The windows are cracking.

We march in like a group of massive spiders,
Strong like a brick wall,
Clashing armour,
Metal boots, sturdy and solid like rocks.

Using a battering-ram to bang down the doors,
Crumbling away,
The rusty metal door handles, getting loose,
Bang! They fall to the hard, stone floor.

Drawing our razor-sharp blades,
Battling millions of soldiers,
Slicing off body parts.
Who will win the battle?

Keeley Bell (11)
Holy Trinity CE Primary School

The Battle

Pitch-black as soot,
We creep quietly to the gate,
The storm growing louder and louder,
The rain crashing down,
Our hopes are high.

Towering above us,
Like a tall mountain,
The castle stands still,
The defiance of the enemy,
Who hopefully are going to lose.

Below the mountain of the castle,
Are the colony of ants,
Waiting to start the battle,
To win something for the their queen.

Boom!
The door screams,
Being bullied.
'*Oohh!*' it cries.
Finally it gives in the tough battle
Of protection for its owners.

Argh!
The screams like owls flood the battlements,
The swords clanging,
The war cries loud,
Running past while dodging silver stars.

More and more soldiers fill the battlements.
I think this means defeat.

Amy Suttling (11)
Holy Trinity CE Primary School

The Wheelchair

A single child's chair,
Empty, lonely,
Round, bright wheels outstanding and large,
A life misunderstood,
Gloomy and under-thought about,
Separated, outcast,
Caged and caught,
Trapped,
Unable and shielded,
Sucked from a world of happiness and understanding,
Never thought of as a person but as a chair,
A loss so deep not to be compared,
Unwanted pity expands and hurts,
Never to smile,
Never to run,
Always to be dark, gloomy and stormy.

But yet . . .

A clearing opens,
Happiness expands,
A light burns and brightens someone's life,
More understood,
Seen more as a person than a chair,
Help on offer,
Complications undone,
More comfortable and calm,
Knots of darkness undone opening to hope,
Reborn at last.

Linzi White (11)
Holy Trinity CE Primary School

The Castle

Windy, dark as a piece of coal.
The night gusts like a monster's breath.

Castle as still as a shark,
About to attack.
Gates are shut like a bear.

We approach like a school of killer whales,
Waiting for the battle to begin.

Clashing feet, cannons bursting out
With metal balls.

Arrows like shooting rockets
In the dark, misty sky.

Hitting balls, loud sounds, waving arms,
Shouting like bees from a hive.

They leave the castle.
Stopped.

Lauren Henderson (11)
Holy Trinity CE Primary School

I'm A Ballerina

I'm a graceful, leapin', twirlin',
hoppin', applaudin', swannin', toe-pointin',
swayin', whirlin', smilin'
to jazz, modern or classic music blarin'
tutu-wearin', lace-crossin'
arm-wavin', hand-holdin',
scurryin', spinnin'
et un, et deux, et trois, et quatre
splits, plié, tights
et cinq, et six, et sept, et huit
tights, plié, splits
I'm a performer
I'm a ballerina!

Joy Young (10)
Maldon Primary School

I Am A Bully

I am a bully.
I am tough, rough and fierce.
I am bold, powerful and evil like a cobra.
I am nasty, stupid and brave.
I am a stolen lunch box,
a broken nose
and an evil ghost.
I am a swooping bat with an evil cry
that pierces the night until the morning.
I am a hunting hawk with flaming eyes.
I fear police sirens but love the sight of blood and gore.
you can't get rid of me.
I am one thing, no, not two,
just the one, never two at all.
I am a terrifying monster.
Ha! Ha!
I am a bully.

James-Morgan Dee (10)
Maldon Primary School

I Am A Victim

I am a victim of bullying.
I am a nobody,
searching,
in hope of a friend.
I am scared and I feel like I am going insane.
I am a rat having my eyes scratched out.
I am a waterfall of tears.
I am like a slithering snake, held in captivity.
I am a trembling coward.
I am wrapped in a blanket of mean reality.
I am a nobody.
I am a victim of bullying.

Charlotte Johnson (10)
Maldon Primary School

I Am A Bully

I am a bully,
rough, tough and powerful like a bear.
I am brave and I am in control.
I have a heart of stone.
I care for no one.
I care for nothing.
I creep, leap and pounce.
I am evil.
I am like a bad penny.
I never go away.
I am a punch in the dark.
I am your worst nightmare.
I am a bully.

Tom Willey (11)
Maldon Primary School

I Am A Bully

I am a bully.
I am nasty, mean and cheeky.
I spy, creep and pull hair.
I am a push into the swimming pool,
a push off the trim trail.
I am awful and spiteful.
I am a pinch, a fight and a twist.
I am a cut arm, thrown stones
and a broken bone.
I am a bully.

Lauren Connolly (9)
Maldon Primary School

I Am A Victim

I am a victim.
I cry.
I shake.
I am scared to go back to school.
I am hunted.
I am a pussy cat.
I am scared to go back to school
Down the corridors.
I am so hopeless.
I am a baby.
I am scared to tell my mum.
I am scared to tell anyone.
They never stop.
I am a pussy cat.
I am a victim.

Jessica Waterman (11)
Maldon Primary School

I Am A Bully

I am a bully.
I am tough, rough and cool.
I punch, kick and shout like a roaring lion.
I hide, sneak and swoop like a bird of prey.
I am a stomach ache before school,
a black eye,
a pain in the neck.
I am a bully.

Fleur Young (10)
Maldon Primary School

I Am A Bully

I am a bully.
I am tough, horrible and mean.
I am in control and hateful.
I am as powerful as a lion.
I steal, betray and I pounce on my victim.
I punch, kick and thump.
I am a demon to my victims -
a devil in flesh and blood.
I am a threat for money,
a kick in the stomach.
I am the black eye.
I am the caved-in nose.
I am lost teeth.
I am the cause of the tear.
I am a bully.

Daniel Billing (11)
Maldon Primary School

I Am A Bully

I am a bully.
I am nasty, terrible and spiteful.
I am unbeatable, awful and tough.
I annoy, call names and steal.
I fight, copy and ambush.
I am a pulled hair.
I am a strangled neck.
I am a bruised leg.
I am a bully.

Iain Buchanan (8)
Maldon Primary School

I Am A Victim

I am a victim.
I am as scared as a field mouse
being approached by a snake.
I am weak.
I am marooned on an island surrounded by sharks.
I am a cracked acorn.
I am a victim of bullying.

Sam Jeffries (11)
Maldon Primary School

As I Walked Along The Beach . . .

As I walked along the beach . . .
The moon kissed the sky
And the sand listened to the tide.
As I walked along the beach . . .
I heard the sun remind the day
Of the dawn that guides the evening.
As I walked along the beach . . .
I heard the sea cry to the stones
And I saw the stone dream in its bed.

Grace Highton (11)
Maldon Primary School

I Am A Victim

I am a victim.
I am scared, creeped and hurt.
I am quiet, cross and cornered.
I creep, spy and cry.
I run, hide and nurse.
I am a squeaking mouse.
I am a victim.

George Jones (9)
Maldon Primary School

Football Freaks

Come on, England,
You're the best,
You can beat all the rest,
Pass the ball, back and forth,
We also have to travel north,
To watch you play,
We hope it goes your way.

A fight breaks out at the England end,
A policeman comes to apprehend,
'Yo, ho, ho', the policeman cries,
'What's going on? And don't tell lies.
Are you stupid or can't you see?
That man has fallen and hurt his knee.'

The policeman said, 'Are you OK?
We'd better get you a good X-ray.'
And although he had tried
To see the final goal,
He found himself in a very deep hole.

The crowd gives out a mighty roar,
As into the net the ball did soar,
Owen grinned from ear to ear,
But all the other team could do was sneer.
The scored turned 3-1,
As the ball goes as fast as gun.

Aaron South (11)
Maldon Primary School

My Friendly Friend

A friend is like a tree
Giving me shade
A friend is like a light
Always shining bright
My best friend.

Aidan Moore (7)
Melbourne Park Primary School

A Friend Is . . .

A friend is there for me
A friend is glad
A friend sticks up for me
And never is she sad.
A friend is bright and never lies
She makes me glad
So very glad.
A friend is a flower
A rose, a red, red rose
And wears pretty clothes.
A friend is there
That is what a friend is for.

Lucy Bearcroft (7)
Melbourne Park Primary School

Friend

A friend helps you up.
A friend is a friend.
A friend is a nice person.
A friend is kind.
A friend is a diamond.
A friend is a star.
My friend is my best friend.

Christopher McDonald (8)
Melbourne Park Primary School

Friend Is For Life

My friend is like a heart
I never give up my spirit
Because she's always at my side
We laugh and laugh until
Our hearts feel like they'll stop
We are friends for life.

Katie Williams (7)
Melbourne Park Primary School

Friendship

Friendship is a powerful force,
Almost as powerful as a horse.
Everyone needs at least one friend,
Without a friend your heart won't mend.

If you want to be a good friend,
You always need to share.
If you do that,
Your friends will care.

Show your friends some respect,
And they will respect you back.
If you want your friendship to last,
You should follow their track.

Don't let your friends boss you around,
Don't let them take charge of you.
If they try and do that,
Put a spider in their shoe.

Latoya Smith (11)
Melbourne Park Primary School

My Friends Are My Cats

I stroke them
They stretch their backs
I play with them
They turn their heads quickly
I feed them
They just rush in
When they are tired
I carry them upstairs
And they curl up on my bed
My cats are my best friends.

Ryan Moore (8)
Melbourne Park Primary School

Friends Are Fun

Friends are fun,
Enjoying the sun.

You have friends,
They are kind.

You play with them,
They play with you.

So enjoy having friends
And your life will end happily.

Don't break your friendship up,
Stay the way you are
And you will have the best friend
That you ever had.

They will care for you,
You care for them.

And share your secrets with them,
And if you have no friends your life will end sadly.

Holly Rainbird (10)
Melbourne Park Primary School

A Friend

A friend is nice
A friend is spice
A friend is sad
A friend is glad
A friend is tall
A friend is small
A friend is light
That lights up the dark
A friend is a state
That's always late.

That's a true friend.

Stephanie Giarnese (8)
Melbourne Park Primary School

My Best Friend

My friends are beautiful
Just like me
We are pretty as a flower
Just as a bee
We are so lovely
It makes me as happy
As a bumblebee
My friend is nice as a heart
A friend that listens to you
Friend, friend, friend
My two best friends.

Sharrel Devenish (8)
Melbourne Park Primary School

My Best Friend

Friend
Friend
Friend
My friend is a light that shines
My friend is a big tree that is lovely
Friend
Friend
Friend
My best friend.

Tayla Peel (7)
Melbourne Park Primary School

My Friend

My friend is a diamond
Because she is beautiful.
My friend is like a beautiful fairy.
My friend is very colourful.
I like my friend.

Lorna Dunn (8)
Melbourne Park Primary School

Friends Forever

Friendship is when you share and care
But don't fight like a bear.

Friendship is as hard as a rock,
You can't break a friendship.

Friendships are fun,
We all like buns.

Don't fight like a bear,
Friends should share and care.

Keep a friendship sweet,
It will live longer than a sheep.

Paige Harlow (10)
Melbourne Park Primary School

A Friend Is Like . . .

A friend is like a flower
It keeps you happy
A friend stands up for you
A friend is like a star that lights up
A friend is good in all ways
And is there for you
Friends look out for each other.

Jordan Brown (7)
Melbourne Park Primary School

Always There

My friend is there
Like a pear
Sparkling in the sky
I must fly and say goodbye.

Josh Ripton (7)
Melbourne Park Primary School

Friendship Is . . .

F riends.
R espect.
I n the best people.
E veryone has more than one friend.
N obody has to be unfriendly to their friends.
D o not let people upset you.
S tand up if you're caught doing something.
H ang around with your friends.
I have got some friends to play with.
P eople like you because you care for them.

Reece Babij (8)
Melbourne Park Primary School

The Best Friend In The . . .

My friend is like a Tudor lady
My friend is like a dog playing with me
My friend
Friend
Friend
Is the best friend in the world.

Claire Barker (7)
Melbourne Park Primary School

Friendship

Guardian angel from above,
Please protect the friend I love,
Met you as a stranger,
Took you as a friend,
Hope to meet in Heaven,
Where friendship never ends.

Demi Elles (10)
Melbourne Park Primary School

Friendship

F riends
R eliable friends
I nteresting friends
E njoyable friends
N oble friends
D elightful friends
S illy friends
H igh friends
I mportant friends
P oppe's friends.

Poppe Johnson (10)
Melbourne Park Primary School

Friendship Poem

F riendship.
R esponsible.
I   really like having friends.
E njoyable.
N ice and kind.
D ecorations.
S haring things.
H aving fun while we play.
I mportant thing to do for your friends.
P arties.

Nicola Peters (10)
Melbourne Park Primary School

Friendship

Friendship is when you share,
Friendship is when you care,
Friendship is when you play together
Friendship is when you help
Friendship is when you work together.

Nyomie Vaughan (11)
Melbourne Park Primary School

Friendship

F riends play with you.
R espect you all the time.
I have fun with my friends.
E veryone has fun with friends.
N eed friends all the time.
D ogs play together in the park.
S ome people have enemies who become friends.
H omeless people need friends to keep them company.
I have friends.
P eople need friends.

Michael Hunt (10)
Melbourne Park Primary School

Friendship

F riends to play with you
R espect you all the time
I have fun with my friends
E veryone has fun together
N eed friends all the time
D ogs have fun together
S ome boys and girls need friends too
H ave friends to take to a café together
I have lots of friends
P eople need friends too.

Scott Bond (9)
Melbourne Park Primary School

Friendship Poem

I like the smell of my best friend's cooking.
I like the feel of my friendly, cuddly, teddy bear.
I like the sound of my friend's bird in its cage cheeping.
I like the look of my friend's baby kitten.
I like the taste of my nan's roast chicken.

Liam Fitzgeorge (8)
Melbourne Park Primary School

Friendship

F riendship is forever,
R eal friends are the best,
I love to have friends,
E verlasting friendship,
N ever forget who your friends are,
D o your best with friendship,
S hare your feelings with each other,
H aving friends is great,
I love to have friends,
P eople who are kind.

Danni Walsh (10)
Melbourne Park Primary School

Friendship

F riends.
R eliable friends.
I nteresting friends.
E njoyable people.
N oble people.
D ependable friends.
S illy friends.
H appy people.
I ntelligent friends.
P eople who care.

Kelly Stratford (11)
Melbourne Park Primary School

My Friend Poem

My friend is good at keep secrets.
My friend is good at playing games.
My friend is good at being kind to me
And he listens to me when I am speaking.

William Prince (9)
Melbourne Park Primary School

Friendship Poem

F riendly,
R eliable,
I ntelligent,
E njoyable,
N ice,
D ependable,
S haring,
H elpful,
I nteresting,
P eople.

Steven Cox (10)
Melbourne Park Primary School

Friendship

F riend
R elationship
I want friends
E very nice friend
N ice
D o not be bored
S mile at friends
H ave fun
I need friends
P lease be polite.

Joshua Kendall (10)
Melbourne Park Primary School

Friendship

A friend is a person who always stays with me
We always play together
We laugh together as well as playing
And also we like to make and break Lego cars together
And also cry together.

Andrew Blanc (10)
Melbourne Park Primary School

Friendship Poem

F riends are people who make you laugh.
R eliable people who you can trust.
I nstead of people you don't.
E nding friendship will never be.
N ever break up with friends.
D on't break up with friends.
S till you will have other friends.
H oping you will have lots of friends.
I will have lots of friends.
P erhaps you will too!

Aaron Khadbai (8)
Melbourne Park Primary School

I Like People

I like people that are nice to me
People who are kind to me
I like people who play with me.

I like people who are nice to me
People who are kind to me
I like people who play games with me
These people are my friends.

Keeley Hull (9)
Melbourne Park Primary School

Friend Poem

A friend is best of all
They make you happy all the time
They are special to you
They may be big or small
But they are still your friend
They have to be nice to you
And they should respect you
And you should too.

Bradley Daly
Melbourne Park Primary School

Friendship Poem

A friend is someone who you can trust and play with all the time.
A friend is someone you can talk to.
A friend is someone who is positive.
A friend is someone who is truthful and helpful.
A friend is someone with a good attitude.
A friend is someone who cheers you up when you are unhappy.
A friend is someone who respects and cares about you.
A friend is someone who shares with you.
A friend is someone who keeps in touch.
A friend is someone who loves you.

Liam Smith (8)
Melbourne Park Primary School

A Friendship Poem

Friends at school play with you and are helpful.
Friends at home are funny and care for you in every way.
Friends at the park are faithful and kind.
Friends at school cheer me up and are company and keep a deal.
Friends on holiday make you feel safe always.
Friends at home laugh when I tell jokes most of the time.
Friends are the best of all!

Charlotte Foster (8)
Melbourne Park Primary School

Friendship Poem

Friends at school are very cool.
Friends at school are kind and helpful.
Friends on holiday are playful and positive.
Friends at parties are sunny and truthful.
Friends at farms are kind.
Friends at school are very cool.

George Chittock (8)
Melbourne Park Primary School

My Best Friend

A friend is a person who likes you,
You like them too.
A friend is like a shadow
Who follows you around.
A friend is someone who shares money with you
And they go without.
A friend is someone who phones you
Day by day.
A friend is someone who sticks up for you.

Amill-Mal Rourke (9)
Melbourne Park Primary School

Friendship Poem

A friend is someone who cares for you
When you are down.

When someone is horrible to you
They will give them a frown.

Friends are nice
They never break up twice.

Edson Clarke (10)
Melbourne Park Primary School

Family

F is for fun, what families are
A is for always, they'll keep you from harm
M is for money, they work hard to earn
I is for interesting, they help you to learn
L is for loving, that they are to me
Y is for you and your family.

Jenny Carter (11)
Melbourne Park Primary School

Friendship

Friends at school
are positive with a good attitude.

Friends at school
keep a promise forever.

Friends at school
are faithful to each other.

Friends at school
trust each other.

Friends at school
care for each other.

Friends at school
are helpful.

Friends at school
are best of all.

Abigail Loble (9)
Melbourne Park Primary School

A Friendship Poem

F riendship is like a butterfly
R emaking friends forever.
I think friendship is really special
E verlasting, it never goes away.
N ever does a friend go away.
D oes it ever go away?
S eeing friends nearly every day.
H earing from them every day.
I love having friendships.
P erfect every day, all the way.

Louiscia McLeod (8)
Melbourne Park Primary School

My Friend

My friend is a star bursting ever so bright.
She is a tiger with ever such might.
She's like a heart pounding ever so strong.
My friend and I are the best of friends.
My friend never lets me down.
She's like a beautiful butterfly with sparkling wings.
We will be friends for
Ever
And
Ever
And
Ever
My friend
Is a flower
In fact, the most beautiful flower.

My friend.

Shannon O'Toole (10)
Melbourne Park Primary School

Friendship

F riends are cool.
R eal friends are kind.
I n the playground they stick up for me.
E very day they play with me.
N ever leave me alone.
D on't break up with me.
S tars in the sky.
H appy friends.
I like my friends.
P lay with them every day.

Emma Bearcroft (9)
Melbourne Park Primary School

My Friend Shannon

My friend is someone who cares for you,
Sticks up for you,
Shares time with you.
My friend is someone who looks out for you,
Walks past with you
And stays with you
Like a rose
For ever and ever.
My friend talks to me
And looks after me
And wherever I go
My friend Shannon will always stay
No matter what.
If she is away on holiday
Shannon is still with me
Because she is
My best friend.

Friends are cool.

Danielle Stimpson (10)
Melbourne Park Primary School

Friends

Friends are always there for you
When you are feeling down.

Friends
Always care for you
When you start to frown.

Friends
Like to share with you
Their new stuff from town.

Sarah Gruneberg (11)
Melbourne Park Primary School

A Friend Is A . . .

Kind, nice person who listens to you,
Stands up for you,
Plays with you,
Helps you when you're stuck,
Looks after you,
Believes in you.

Jack Ryan (10)
Melbourne Park Primary School

My Musical Friend

I've got a
Musical friend
Who makes me laugh.
He sings like a star
And the girls think he is
A musical red
And most beautiful
Rose.

Levi-Wayne Stanley (7)
Melbourne Park Primary School

Friendship

A friend is someone
Who cares for you
And is there for you.
When I'm feeling sad
He will cheer me up.
How will the world be
Without a friend?

Ahmed Karim (10)
Melbourne Park Primary School

A Friendship Poem

If you have a problem, a friend is always kind,
A friend is someone who you can always find.
Friends stick up for you,
Old friends or new.

Friends are people that always play,
Play and play and play all day.
Friends sometimes look like they gleam,
Good friends are friendly and that mine seem.

They're always there,
Always care,
They always play fair.
Sometimes with you build a secret lair.
You break up and you make up!

Best friends.

Ellie Rose Folkard (8)
Melbourne Park Primary School

My Parents

There once was a woman named Dee
Who said she always wanted to be
An office adviser
Have a girl called Elisa,
But unfortunately she only got me.

My dad, he's a brilliant parent
But there is one thing that I daren't -
It'd be to swear
And not to care
In front of another parent.

My dad, he's a brilliant guy.
At football he always would try
To give his all
While kicking the ball,
When he misses he always will sigh.

Ben Hastings (11)
Melbourne Park Primary School

A Friend

A friend is someone,
Who cares for you,
Sticks up for you,
Shares with you.

A friend is someone,
Who laughs with you,
Walks paths with you,
Hurrahs with you,
That's a good friend.

Not a friend is someone,
Who bullies you,
Pushes you,
And it hurts too.

Not a friend is someone,
Who calls you names,
Not playing games,
I know I wouldn't want a friend like that.

Leah Kirby (9)
Melbourne Park Primary School

Friendships

Friendships are like a chain that cannot be broken.
A friendship is like a puzzle that fits together for ever and ever
And will always play every day.
A friendship has to have at least two to make it true
And there's only one more thing you have to be
Like two peas in a pod.

Jade Turner (10)
Melbourne Park Primary School

Best Friends

Friends are kind
Because they have a mind.
They help us find things
When they are lost.
Friends cheer us up
When we are sad.
Where would we be
Without our friends?

Harry Sharp (9)
Melbourne Park Primary School

Friendship

A friend is kind,
A friend is loyal,
A friend can find
Your tin foil.
A friend will give you a card
When you have landed
On a glass shard.

Jonathon Russell (9)
Melbourne Park Primary School

My Best Friend

My best friend calls me every day, day, day.
She speaks to me on the phone.
If I go round I have to shut the gate.
She looks into my eyes.
She is the one who looks out for me,
Cares for me.

Katie Turner-Wright (9)
Melbourne Park Primary School

Best Friend

A friend is like a sun
And smiles like a mum
And is always there
To keep you company.
When you're sad
They come and play.
They never, never let you down.
They always care
And let you round.
If you're hurt
They will help you up.
They support you
Whatever you're going through.
If you're being bullied
They stand up for you.
That is what a friend is for.

Mary-Louise Harrington (9)
Melbourne Park Primary School

Friends

Friends are the best.
Recognise them all.
I have a friend who is small.
Even if I have a small friend
Never, ever will my friendship end.
Day by day, speak to my friends
Saying how are you?
Tell me at the end.

Naomi Toublic (9)
Melbourne Park Primary School

Best Friend

A friend is a sunflower to me
Because they are so kind to me
And they are so helpful.
That is why they're my friends.

Curtis Devenish (9)
Melbourne Park Primary School

I'm A . . .

Horse ridin', ground shakin',
Baby wakin', law breakin',
Show jumpin', crowd makin',
Gorse eatin', trophy winnin',
Tree squashin', cheer leadin',
Zoo escapin', fruit stealin',
Violet movin', race winnin',
Horse.
I also like:
Heavy hoofin', grass choppin',
Lawn mowin', hair flyin',
Crowd sweepin', heavy sleepin',
Fast eatin', gulp drinkin',
Clip cloppin', high jumpin',
Speedy sprintin', fence breakin',
Snake chasin', hay chompin',
Mud flyin', bark spreadin',
Loud neighin', sound bearin',
Best biggest horse!

Claudia Sandford-Bates (10)
Millfields Primary School

Best Buddy

She's funny
She's funky
She's bouncy and jumpy.

She's fluffy
She's furry
She's soft and silky.

She's noisy
She's smart
She's cute and cuddly.

She's speedy
She's fit
She's warm and sleepy.

My best buddy
Is
My cat.

Emily Hirst (10)
Millfields Primary School

Where Does A Monster Live?

A monster lives
Under your bed
In your wardrobe
Up your chimney
In the bin
Down the toilet
In the car
Up the curtains
In your shower
Down the play
In the floor
On the roof
That's where a monster lives.

George Fisher (10)
Millfields Primary School

On The Catwalk

C ome, come, see the show.

A t the hall on the catwalk, come, come, see the show.

T onight at the hall on the catwalk, come, come, see the show.

W ow! Look at that dress, tonight at the hall on the catwalk, come, come, see the show.

A bright orange pair of trousers. Oh my word! Wow! Look at that dress, tonight at the hall on the catwalk, come, come, see the show.

L ong T-shirts with a bright orange pair of trousers. Oh my word! Wow! Look at that dress, tonight at the hall on the catwalk, come, come, see the show.

K nock, knock, their heels make, long T-shirts with a bright orange pair of trousers. Oh my word! Wow! Look at that dress, tonight at the hall on the catwalk, come, come, see the show.

Harriet Scott (10)
Millfields Primary School

The Skeleton On The Toilet

We live in Nottage in a small cottage
And the biggest room is the bathroom.
Nobody goes there, not even me, but I stay in my bedroom.
Now there's a reason, a reason why, even though I try to avoid
But once it happened to nobody but me.
My tummy was rumbling, do you see?
I needed the toilet so very much, I grabbed a stick for a crutch!
My tummy was rumbling, I needed to go.
I was so desperate but I couldn't show.
So I ran to the bathroom, now what did I see?
A skeleton on the toilet, staring at me!

Charlotte Fern Bryan (10)
Millfields Primary School

Monkey Shadows

I wish I were a monkey in the jungle
Swinging from tree to tree happily
The jungle is my home

I wish I was a monkey in the jungle
The jungle is very noisy with loads of
Creatures and animals talking

I wish I was a monkey in the jungle
Talking and playing with the monkeys all day

I wish I was a monkey in the jungle
I have a very furry tail. My tail makes me
Jump high and from tree to tree

I wish I was a monkey in the jungle
Eating fruit all day long in the trees
On the floor, in my den

I just wish I was a monkey in the jungle.

James Coppin (7)
Millfields Primary School

Shark Shadows

I wish I was a shark that was very strong in the deep blue sea
I would dart place to place faster than a motorbike catching prey

I would go close to shore and wait . . . until the right moment, and then,
I would pounce on the humans and gobble them all up

I would stop other things as dangerous as a tiger from
Coming into shark territory.
I would protect it all day
From twelve in the morning to twelve at night.

Thomas Liddy (8)
Millfields Primary School

People

There are lots of different people in the world,
Funny, cool or weird.
Some people have moustaches
And old people have beards.

Some girls are pretty
And some are spotty and strange.
Some have afro hair
And some girls have it straight.

A lot of boys like football
But some prefer cards,
Some boys find maths easy,
Some find it hard.

Parents are the worst
Telling you off all the time.
Do this, do that,
Whine, whine, whine.

Everyone is different,
That can't ever change.
Accept the way you are
Whether you are normal or strange.

Chelsea Duce (10)
Millfields Primary School

The Bomb

There once was a good boy called Tom
Who lived on top of a bomb
When it went boom poor Tom's head flew
And went off like a ball
And landed in my room.

Alex Tierney (9)
Millfields Primary School

Animal Alphabet

A is for Ant
B is for Bat
C is for Cat
D is for Dog
E is for Elephant
F is for Fish
G is for Goat
H is for Hamster
I is for Iguana
J is for Jellyfish
K is for Kangaroo
L is for Leopard
M is for Monkey
N is for Newt
O is for Octopus
P is for Pelican
Q is for Quail
R is for Rabbit
S is for Snake
T is for Tiger
U is for Unicorn
V is for Vote
W is for Whale
X is Impossible
Y is for Yeti
Z is for Zebra.

Hannah Nelson (10)
Millfields Primary School

Dog Shadows

I wish I was a dog in the wild
Sprinting through the fresh air of
The open wild

I wish I was a dog in the wild
Howling and playing just like all
The other animals in the wild

I wish I was a dog in the wild
Wrestling in the leaves with bright
Teeth as sharp as a razor

I wish I was a dog in the wild
Galloping over lots of lovely brown
Golden tree trunks

I wish I was a dog in the wild
Screaming and crying in laughter.

Matty Duce (8)
Millfields Primary School

Kiwis

The kiwi, the kiwi as much as it tries,
The kiwi, the kiwi it just cannot fly.
The kiwi, you see, it doesn't have wings,
But the kiwi, the kiwi can do other things.

The kiwi, the kiwi has a beak a foot long,
The kiwi, the kiwi has a strange song.
The kiwi, the kiwi has so much fun,
The kiwi, the kiwi lies in the sun.

The kiwi, the kiwi is a bird that lays eggs,
The kiwi, the kiwi has very small legs.
Who cares that the kiwi, the kiwi can't fly?
'Cause the kiwi, the kiwi's a friend to you and I.

Robbie Taylor Hunt (10)
Millfields Primary School

Lion Shadows

I wish I were a lion in the Sahara desert

Cautiously I'd prance about on paws as big as frying pans
I'd growl angrily at my enemies

I wish I were a lion in the Sahara desert
My eyes would shimmer in the sunlight
In the plains of the Sahara desert I'd be happy

If I were a lion in the Sahara desert
I'd doze in my den
With tooth sharp claws
I'd hunt elephants at dusk

I'd tear my bait apart viciously
And I'd eat
My glimmering hair would swish about in the summer air
My damp nose would twitch in all directions
I'd play hide-and-seek in the grass
With the other animals

My eyes would gaze happily around me
I'd be king of the desert

While hunters search for me miles away
I'd creep away to my secret domain
I'd dream a lions dream.

Laurel Regibeau (8)
Millfields Primary School

I Wish I Was A Dolphin

I wish I was a dolphin in the swishing and swishing sea
I'd jump out of the water and then dive back in
I wish I was a dolphin

I wish I was a dolphin in the swishing and swirling sea
When I jump out of the water
Water would spray from me

I wish I was a dolphin in the swishing and swishing sea.

Louisa Theeman (7)
Millfields Primary School

Wolf Shadows

I wish I was a wolf in the Pyrenees mountains
The mountains would be my friends

I would growl all day
Hunting for my prey
In the icy snow
Of the Pyrenees mountains

I wish I was a wolf in the Pyrenees mountains
My paws as big as small paint tins
Padding down on the icy snow

I wish I was a wolf in the Pyrenees mountains
I would see blood as red as the mill fields
Spilt on the ground

When I'm happy my tail is as wiggly as jelly
But when I'm sad my tail is as stiff as ice.

I would curl up in my rocky den and fall fast asleep
Oh I wish I was a wolf in the Pyrenees mountains.

Alfred Twyman (7)
Millfields Primary School

Romans Don't Wear Underpants

Romans wear steel helmets
Gold brooches and
Iron shields
But Romans don't wear underpants

Romans wear wool tunics
Chain mail and
Leather shoes
But Romans don't wear underpants!

Romans wear big feathers
Thick wool and
Steel armour
But Romans don't wear *underpants.*

Bill Twyman (10)
Millfields Primary School

At School

Sitting at my desk
In the middle of a test.
It's so boring
Pupils snoring
In the middle of a test.

In my head the bell is ringing, pupils flinging school
Bags over their back, running around several blocks
Finally home, flinging open the door,
Then just check the football score,
Running out of the door again,
Going to the park to meet a friend,
Playing on the swings
And doing fun things.
Then I hear a voice saying, 'Billy, Billy, don't be silly'
Then it all comes back to me
To the place as boring as can be
Looking into each sleeping face and thinking
Get me out of this place!

Miriam Clavane (8)
Millfields Primary School

Blue Whale Shadows

I wish I was a blue whale in the sea
The sea would be my friend

I would go to the bottom of the sea and find
The fattest, juiciest fish with one big swish

I would swim a thousand metres before
I run out of breath
I would jump out of the sea
Like a firework shooting into the sky

I wish I was a blue whale in the sea.

James Blanchette (8)
Millfields Primary School

Dolphin Shadows

I wish I was a dolphin in the splashing silver water
Flipping my fins in the silver water
People would throw all kinds of fish
Out in the sea for me to eat

I wish I was a dolphin in a metallic blue sea
Jumping about till midnight in the sunset
With the blue waves spreading the sky

I wish I was a dolphin
Prancing and dancing deep in the foamy blue water
I would dance with the turtles, jellyfish, and octopus
And all kinds of fish

I wish I was a dolphin
Jumping as high as the moon
Visiting loads and loads of planets
Like the galaxy and Mars and Milky Way, eating them up
For my drink I will have some water from the sea

I wish I was a dolphin swimming through
Into the underwater kingdom
With the underwater king
With his dolphin guarded throne.

Mia Krikler (8)
Millfields Primary School

We All Got Rhythm

Rhythm in a rocking chair
Rocking to and fro
Rhythm in your singing when you tone it high to low
Rhythm when you're sleeping and you do not make a sound
Rhythm in your dancing as you gently skip around
Everything you do has a fast or slow beat to it
It doesn't need a backing track it just needs you to do it!

Petra Jones (10)
Millfields Primary School

I Wish I Was A Dolphin

I wish I was a dolphin in the sea like
A saucepan swimming, floating gently and
Swiftly in the tide

Everyone will look at me swimming beautifully
In between those mean looking sharks

If I were a dolphin in the sea everything
Around would be like a dream

The surface would be my breath for air
And the shark enemies that I can
Easily beat

I wish I was a dolphin in the sea
I would splash in and out of the
Waves it would be glory

If I were a dolphin in the sea
I could talk to the people on boats
And sing to the people
Like a hummingbird.

Rebecca Hart (7)
Millfields Primary School

Do Pigs Fly?

Do pigs fly or do they not?
Is it an expression or is it not?
Pigs try to fly they never do
They drive planes, that's not enough
They wear glasses, that's not true
They play poker they have a clue
They still can't match the flying pig
So that's what pigs do
They still can't fly
They will still try.

Chippy Clarke (10)
Millfields Primary School

My Best Friend

My best friend Tom lives in a nuclear bomb
He likes to sing
He never puts anything in the bin
He sings like a ding a-ling a-ling
His dad is the king
He loves to cling to the edge of the bin
His dad is very thin
His names is King Bush
Yesterday he had to push the car
And opened the door with a crowbar
He likes to play with his grandma
His favourite car is a Ferrari
His favourite food is salami
He's very barmy his brother's in the army
His eyes are blue he has new shoes
He likes to lose he likes to choose
His new shoes.

Dayle Martyn Foreman (10)
Millfields Primary School

Cheetah Shadows

I wish I was a cheetah in the African plain
Hunting would be my teacher

I would lay in the shade in the day
Like cows in a field
In the evening I would hunt
And I would

I would catch prey and go as fast
As a Harrier jump jet

I would have teeth as sharp as a blade
And hunt the gazelles and antelope
I wish I was a cheetah.

Tom Connery (8)
Millfields Primary School

Sport Mad

Sport is fun
Pool is quiet
Orienteering is adventurous
Running is cool
Tennis great

Mountain climbing is freezing and cold
Athletics is tiring
Dog racing is quick

This is what I think of sport!

Jake Toby Hughes (10)
Millfields Primary School

Eagles

Soar with an eagle
In the shiny sky
Jump off mountains
And then start to fly

Soar with an eagle
On a night sky
They can jump
And soar very high.

Samuel Williamson (8)
Millfields Primary School

Mr Men And Little Miss

There's Mr Lazy who is so crazy
And there's Mrs Small standing next to Mr Tall
Mr Grumpy always has his tea lumpy
There's Little Miss Shy who's eating lemon pie
And there's Little Miss Trouble who wants
To give you a cuddle, and don't forget
Mr Greedy who always eats kiwi.

Emma O'Neill (9)
Northwick Park Junior School

My Best Friend

My best friend looks exactly like me
She's got brown hair and eyes like me
But her hair's as long as the Nile
And also she hates tea
She's got five special feathers
And seven pairs of shoes
Two six foot wardrobes
And never has some news

She copies every move I make
And copies every sign
She always wears the same as me
And she's always gonna be mine
We seem to get on very well
She looks quite familiar
But only then did I notice that
My best friend was a mirror.

Hollie-Ann Boomer (10)
Northwick Park Junior School

My Day In The Lifetime

I sat upon a seat
And had mud upon my feet
I went home for tea
And my friend played with me
We played on the slide
And had a pony ride
I went to bed
With a sleepy head
Goodnight sleep tight
Don't let the bedbugs bite.

Roni Louise Foyster (9)
Northwick Park Junior School

What

She awoke
As she heard
The lightning
Crashing against
The window
She fell on the floor
As it opened the door
It started stroking her hair
And then
What, who, where?
She let out a scream
What turned out to be a vibration
Which shattered the mirror
The clock started ticking
Tick, tock, tick, tock.

Faye Rogers (9)
Northwick Park Junior School

Whisper From The Wind

Many people's names
Echo through the air
Playing mind games
But we think it's not fair

For why should they be permitted
To toy with our thoughts
The ones that have been fitted
The ones our heart has caught

Many people's names
Echo through the air
Playing mind games
And still it's not fair.

Connar Hobbs (11)
Northwick Park Junior School

Little Miss Naughty

Little Miss Naughty is my name
And she is to blame
For this terrible name
She is to blame

Little Miss Naughty is my name
She is insane
Driving me mad every day
She is insane in every way

Little Miss Naughty is my name
Being naughty is my aim
Go away I'm playing a game
The game you know is not the same

Little Miss Naughty is my name
That's my name
That's my name
Little Miss Naughty is my name.

Shannon Mostyn (10)
Northwick Park Junior School

What I Can Hear And Do

I can see the great outdoor with lovely green, green, grass
All the birds are singing beautifully I can hear them from afar
The shade is quite nice and cool and no one can find me
And in the shade I can see a creepy, crawly centipede
I'll play with my friends all day and we'll have lots of fun
And this day, our day, will last under the sun
The wind is whistling through the grass and singing beautiful
And everyone is asking me what can I see
I can see bugs flying through the air
And, hey look, it's a butterfly fluttering past my hair
Have a try to read my poem of
What I can hear and do.

Ellis Evans (9)
Northwick Park Junior School

Me And My Music

I love to sing whenever I can
I drive Mum mad but she's my biggest fan
I sing in the school choir with my friend Hollie-Ann
I sing in the bath and in front of my nan

I love any music that comes to my hand
I love to play the cornet in my local brass band
We perform lots of concerts all over the land
I won a big trophy it was all very grand

I also play recorder, Miss Goldsmith teaches me at school
It's a good instrument to start with, as it's nice and small
I've played in front of parents and in the church hall
There was a time I hurt my thumb and couldn't play at all

Going to the Cliffs pavilion will be my biggest show
I'm very excited, I can't wait to go
My family will be watching me from the front row
I hope they don't put me off and my voice is not too low

When I grow up, I want a flash car
To own a big house with a fancy Jacuzzi spa
Visit lots of places, travel very far
But most of all, I dream to be a star

When I'm alone at night, thinking about where my life's bound
I lie on my bed and listen to the sound
I thank my lucky stars for the music that I've found
And bless God for the harmony he's given us all around.

Jessica Bronze (10)
Northwick Park Junior School

Cats

Cats are fluffy
Cats are cute
Cats are cuddly
And I have two

Cats are playful
Cats have fun
Cats can climb
Cats can run

Cats have whiskers
Cats have tails
Cats catch birds
But sometimes fail

Cats can sleep
For hours on end
My cats are my
Two best friends.

Jessica Nelson (10)
Northwick Park Junior School

The Dead Of Night

In the dead of night
I get a funny fright
It sounds like ghouls
Running round our schools
It feels like a poisoned rose
Running all round my nose
I feel blood come from my face
I look in the mirror but there's no trace
The mirror breaks I start to scream
Thank goodness for that it's only a dream.

Michaela Bannon (8)
Northwick Park Junior School

My School Is Fun

I like my school
I run through the gates
It's fun and it's cool
My teacher is great

My friends are great fun
We'll be friends forever
We skip, play and run
We like being together

We all eat our lunch
Then pick buttercups and daisies
We pick a big bunch
Then sit down to be lazy

Soon it's time to go home
We've finished our sums
Back through the gates we roam
And get a hug from our mums.

Bethany Barnard (9)
Northwick Park Junior School

Titanic

Titanic is a very big boat
It was so heavy it did not float
'It's time we went,' said everyone,
'Because the day is nearly done.'
'We're nearly there,' some people heard
'Oh no, we've hit a great iceberg!'
And as the great ship snapped in two
The passengers, out they flew
And as all the people lay dead
All you could see was a thousand dead heads.

Jessica Andrews (9)
Northwick Park Junior School

My Dog Polly

My dog Polly plays football with me
You will never get the ball off of her when she's got it

Doing acrobats when the ball has been kicked up high
Of course you will find her amusing
Growling at us because we've gone out

Pulling and pushing her toys like a lion killing its prey
Of course I love her with all my heart, and we will never part
Laughing at her all day,
Laughing can never be the same without her licking me
Stop, stop it *tickles!*
You're truly my best friend.

Amy Hadden (10)
Northwick Park Junior School

Dancing Girl

Dancing girl never stops
Jumping around like a balloon when it pops
Wandering around like she's in a daydream
Shaking her hips with her tambourine
Moving her head with the beat of the music
Doing her hair whilst picking some tulips

Laughing with all the people around her
Saying things like 'hello miss' and 'hello sir'
Prancing around like a cheetah jumping
Walking with the sound of her tap shoes clumping
Living in a life where everyone's happy
Happy when they see the dancing girl!

Holly Barlow (10)
Northwick Park Junior School

The Bears

Monday's bear can bike and ride
Tuesday's bear is always tied
Wednesday's bear plays football
Thursday's bear can climb a tree
Friday's bear is best at cuddles
Saturday's bear gets in muddles
Sunday's bear I'm proud to say
He's just scored a goal *hip hip hooray!*

Elisha Brett (9)
Northwick Park Junior School

A Different Place

In a different empire
There you can see vampires
Also there are witches
There are dirty dishes
Waiting in the room
Witches on their brooms
Creatures with wings
Wolves with tail rings.

Leesha Louise Goody (11)
Northwick Park Junior School

Planets!

I stare through the hole of my telescope
I gaze beyond the stars
I watch Saturn spinning round, and ruby red Mars
I long to seek Jupiter, the titanic one of all
And cold blue Pluto, although it is very small
I gaze at Uranus with its cold icy core
And thank God I'm on earth here for evermore.

Georgia Louise Dean (11)
Northwick Park Junior School

Space

Flying through space
Tying up my face
Don't know where I'll go
But I'm rather slow

Which planet will I visit first?
Mercury, Mars, Neptune
I think I might burst
Jupiter, Pluto, Uranus

I think I might go home now
Back to my own house
Back to the human race
To my own private place.

Thomas Daykin-Woodberry (11)
Northwick Park Junior School

The Midnight Bus

At night when people sleep
The midnight bus drives and drives
It drives at top speed and the driver
Is a ghost called Clive

The midnight bus lets ghosts go in
And it never stops driving
It only stops to let the ghost out

In the morning, the midnight bus fades
And the midnight bus
Returns back at night.

James Cory (10)
Northwick Park Junior School

Big Brother Bear

Big brother bear do you have to go
Can't you stay with me and sissy yo
Please say yes
I'll be the best
I promise
Please stay with us big brother bear

Big brother bear you staying hooray!
You're not going out with your girlfriend May
You're staying here while Mum goes out
Can we go on the roundabout?
Or maybe the swing?
I don't care; you're staying Big Brother Bear.

Kara-Anne Johnston (10)
Northwick Park Junior School

Why?

I'm going to a football stadium
Why?
So I can help Arsenal
Why?
Because I want them to be champions
Why?
Because I want them to beat every team
Why?
They have a lot of skill
Why?
Why don't you stop saying why?
Why?

Jordan Parsons (8)
Northwick Park Junior School

Molly Minton Made A Mustard Melon In A Minute

Molly Minton Made A Mustard Melon In A Minute
If Molly Minton made a mustard melon in a minute
What would it taste like?
Molly Minton ate the mustard melon she made in a minute
Molly Minton said the melon she made in a minute tasted like mustard

Molly Minton made a mustard melon shop in a minute
Molly Minton made a lot of money in a minute
In the mustard melon shop.

Molly Minton (8)
Northwick Park Junior School

My Friend Jamie

My friend Jamie's very small in fact he's only 4 foot tall
He has big brown eyes
And a freckly nose
He's into sport in a very big way
Each night after school we go out to play
We go round each other's houses for tea
And his favourite is spag bol just like me
He's the best friend I've ever had
And if I lost him I'd be very sad.

Paige Quinn (10)
Northwick Park Junior School

Not So Far La Dee Da

The family went off in the car
But oh dear we didn't get very far
The tyre popped and the car just stopped
So we all sang 'La dee da!'

But it was too hard to mend in the end.

Aaron Holmes (8)
Northwick Park Junior School

Flowers

Roses are red
Violets are blue
When I look at you I will miss you

Violets are blue
Roses are red
It feels like I want to go to bed

Grass is green
Mud is black
It feels like a wolf is about to attack.

Molly Rose-Smith (11)
Northwick Park Junior School

Hairy Bear

Once I went to buy a pair of shoes to wear
Then I met a Hairy Bear
Who said:
'Do you want to share my pear?'
'Yes I would like to share
But you gave me a bit of a scare'
'Let's sit over there' said the Bear
'Ok!' I said in fear
'But do not sit too near.'

Sophie Edwards (9)
Northwick Park Junior School

Summer

S un comes out in summer
U nlimited flowers bloom so bright
M orning sun wears out the night
M illions of songs sung by birds
E veryone enjoys the sun, getting a tan and having fun but
R emember winter comes soon so have fun and don't waste summer!

Danielle Winter (10)
Northwick Park Junior School

The Spooky Castle

I went past the shop
And I came up to a grey gate
And ran and saw some poppies
In the grass
And came to a brown door
And I went through a hall
And said 'boo' to the ghost
And came to a stinky wall
And saw a bad rat
With yellow teeth
And came to some steps
And I went through a door
And saw a big spider web
And brushed it off
And I saw a small box
And opened it
And they took the gold key
To the ginormous castle.

Kori Learoyd Tuckwell
Old Heath Primary School

I Wish

This is the star that flashed in the sky
This is the planet that spun in the sky
This is the shooting star that raced up in to the sky
This is the moon that winked at the star
This is the rocket that shot up in the sky
I wish I had a star to share all my secrets.

Holly Lewis
Old Heath Primary School

Clinking Key Castle

The girl went past the sweet shop
And carried on up the path
And came to a groaning gate
And there were pink poppies and green graves
But she passed them
And came to deadly door.
She went in the door
And it led her to a horrible hall.
She went through the hall in to a creepy cellar
There was a red rat.
She said, 'scat'
To the rat
And 'boo'
To the glowing ghost
And brushed the scary spider
And said, 'ha ha'
And took the clicking key to the creaking castle.

Chloe Pudney
Old Heath Primary School

Girls And Boys

A is for Aimee who likes chasing boys
B is for Billy who makes lots of noise
C is for Charlotte who likes cake
D is for David who likes to bake
E is for Emma who is a star
F is for Finley who drives a car
G is for Garry who has a runny nose
H is for Hannah who has smelly toes.

Autumn Tidmarsh (9)
Prettygate Junior School

Silver Trails

Hard shelled and slimy
A mollusc and it's grimy
It's like a spiral with a neck
And a head like my uncle
With a hangover

A caravan with flat tyres
Yet shoots away from fires
Its shell quaking in fear
Of the orange and yellow monster
Coming its way

Then it comes out from hide
Like a tunnel entrance wide
Its mouth a gaping hole
A silent movie actor
Mouthing soundless words
To an invisible friend

It can live nearly anywhere
With its home upon its back
But the one thing that makes it clear
To where a snail has been
It leaves its silver trails
For you and I to see.

Oliver Totham (10)
Prettygate Junior School

The Sun

Rise in the east
And set in the west
Of all the stars that light the sky
Our sun is the best
Up in the morning
Down in to the night
Our sun is burning brightly
And providing our light.

Alex Sutcliffe (9)
Prettygate Junior School

Seal Eater Shark

Deathly silence surrounds it like a shield
It curves its tail
Side to side like a snake
A smell invades its nostrils
Like a great army
Instant speed drives it forward
Like a cheetah
It streaks through the waves
As if they were a blue desert

The evil of its eyes are like fire
Raging throughout its streamlined shape
Teeth like razors
Steel jaws
The silent roar echoes
Blood stains the water like a storm cloud
It finally dives down to the depths and waits after
A satisfying seal meal
A shark it was and it will always be a seal eater.

Taras Kokolski (10)
Prettygate Junior School

Tiger

His black and orange stripes
His swirly long tail
His tiny ears
His big long whiskers
His teeth are like an edge of an open can
Prowling around the jungle
Looking for food to eat
Behind the grass looking at its prey
Pouncing on its prey like a bolt of lightning.

Charlotte Graves (9)
Prettygate Junior School

The Hunter

Guess what I am
I have big stripy stripes
My fur is as soft as sheep's wool
I have a big growling roar
I duck down like a log on the ground

I run like the fastest man on Earth
I hunt for deer and wild snorting pigs
My teeth are tough and sharp to gobble you up
Of course I am as wild as a wicked witch

Guess what I am!
For all that information
I am a *tiger*
Roar . . . roar . . . roar . . .

Amy Ketley (10)
Prettygate Junior School

The Screeching Hawk

The screeching hawk swoops down from its nest
Flying at its very best

It swipes its prey like a magic spell
But the fish almost nearly fell

But the hawk gripped as tight as it could
But the hawk just wouldn't give in

Flying through the windy climate
Trying to keep on course

It returns to its nest breathing at its very best.

Emily Jackson (10)
Prettygate Junior School

Horse

A coat of sunshine, he gallops around
The heavenly greenness of the field
A tail and mane of snow white
Bouncing in the light wind
He is a marvel of clouds and dreams when he runs
The elegant, long legs moving with ease
Jumping grandly over hedges
Yet in the night, when all is quiet
With a warm bunch of hay
He stands there a black marble statue
And as the golden sunset lowers vertical, sleepness drowns
Waiting until morning dawns.

Alice Fawkes (9)
Prettygate Junior School

Red Squirrel

In the early morning
Just when dawn has broken
You see it
Screeching in the sun
As quick as lightning it flies up a tree
Gnawing on a brilliant brown nut
A flaming red bushy rat
Collecting apple green acorns for the winter to come.

Alexander Hindle (10)
Prettygate Junior School

My Little Dinosaur

I jump up to my prey as I run, as I run
I am as small as a chair when I hop, when I hop
My claws are as sharp as a bear when I scratch, when I scratch
My little dinosaur is as fast as a gun being fired
As it runs, as it runs.

Dale Gladwin (9)
Prettygate Junior School

Best Friend Away

My best friend is away
Can't settle down
Always fidgeting about
Always waiting for that call
Always waiting for that shout
'Anna, Abi's on the phone'
Instead I hear my mum's voice
Moan, drone, moan
Part of me is missing
No amount of kissing
From my mum and dad
Can stop me thinking about what I had
I'm awfully lonely without her
Please come back.

Anna Walker (9)
Prettygate Junior School

Snow

When it's cold winter is here
Just think of snow
Cold as ice like white clouds
Soft as a sponge
Smooth as your skin
So fun that you want it to stay
But winter has gone
Still don't get your hopes down
Winter will come again
With lots of snow
But just think about what I said.

Maryam Nadim (9)
Prettygate Junior School

Slimy Snake

Slithering slimy snake
With slivery scaly skin
Sounding like a cat hissing
Hearing like an owl
Big teeth and long body
As long as a car. It lives
In the jungle and wrapping
Its body round like a
Scarf his teeth are poison
Enough to kill you. The
Snake is as blue as the
Sea and it is as smooth
As a mirror.

Daniel Whitmore (10)
Prettygate Junior School

I Know My Cat's An Angel

I know my cat's an angel
For she watches over me
Slyly, when her eyes seem shut
At night when I can't see

I know my cat's an angel
For her ears protect my sleep
A creak, a squeak, a footfall
At any noise she'll leap

I know my cat's an angel . . .

Jemma Whitmore (9)
Prettygate Junior School

Simon The Snake

There was a snake called Simon
Who was very long and scaly
He had a great big appetite
And ate ten mice daily

Simon is a friendly snake
And smiles at passers by
But didn't like the girl next door
And used to make her cry

The girl next door was called Lucy
She hated snakes a lot
One day she grabbed him by the neck
And shoved him in a pot.

Holly Sibley (8)
Prettygate Junior School

A Pig From Peru

He wobbles and runs place to place
Looking for food, drink and shade
Foes are many
Humans, mountain lions, others too
So many . . .
I can't imagine
How he survives
Thin, fat
Many sizes and types he comes . . .

Nathanael Dale (10)
Prettygate Junior School

Sir Ficketty Fox

Sir Ficketty Fox was a little ox
So little he was that he'd lost his fox
Fast as a rat, solid as a box
Was this annoying Sir Ficketty Fox?

His tail was sore, his eyes were small
He wanted to crawl to the enormous hall
Small as an ant, soft as socks
Was this little Sir Ficketty Fox?

Sir Ficketty Fox was a little dude
So hungry he was that he'd lost his food
Cool as a car, safe as locks
Was this cool Sir Ficketty Fox?

Sir Ficketty Fox had a big dam
And his friend owl was called Sam
Smart as a teacher, wet as docks
Was this Sir Ficketty Fox?

James Bouckley (9)
Prettygate Junior School

Fox

A huge shadow creeping around the gardens
Merging with the ground
As it burrows deeper and deeper
To make its small warm home
A rough, red figure hunting its prey
A predator in the dark
When a human comes near
It lightly screeches
Like nails on a blackboard
To scare it away.

Mathew Streeting (10)
Prettygate Junior School

A Is For

A is for Adam who runs very fast
B is for Ben who hates coming last
C is for Charlie who likes making cakes
D is for Daniel who hangs by the lake
E is for Ella who likes new toys
F is for Frankie who likes the boys
G is for Gary who likes painting doors
H is for Hannah who likes knowing more
I is for Iona who likes her name
J is for Jemma who likes playing games
K is for Kerry who likes having fun
L is for Laura who loves a good run
M is for Molly who likes watching telly
N is for Nelly who has a big belly
O is for Olivia who likes to dance
P is for Poppy who likes going to France
Q is for Queenie who has lots of money
R is for Rachel who is very funny
S is for Sophie who is very good
T is for Terry who makes things from wood
U is for Uri who makes things bend
V is for Victor who moans to the end
W is for Wally who can never be found
X is for Xana who jumps up and down
Y is for Yasmin who plays in the park
Z is for Zara who doesn't like the dark.

Abbie Alpine (9)
Prettygate Junior School

Guinea Pig

Scurrying about like a car and scattering
It runs about its cage or garden
And feels like a soft, fluffy teddy
Eating all day - carrots, cucumber
And I see it all the time.

Elizabeth Hampshire (10)
Prettygate Junior School

Football Teams

A is for Arsenal who score lots of goals
B is for Bolton who don't have Paul Scholes
C is for Colchester, which is our hometown
D is for Derby who I hope go down
E is for Everton who are short of a goal
F is for Forest Green; if they spend enough money they'll get Joe Cole
G is for Gillingham who aren't a good team
H is for Hull who always daydream
I is for Islington who walk in the wood
J is for Juventus who are very good.

Nathan Courtier (8)
Prettygate Junior School

Web Foot

The fur of this animal is like a lion's mane
If this animal's pointy beak poked you
As a lion would bite you - *ow!* The pain!
It's wet like it's gone round the whole wide world's water
It catches its prey with a slaughter
The swish movement is like a basketball hitting the net
It would make a strange pet.

Joshua Wright (10)
Prettygate Junior School

Flowers Of The Garden

G is for geraniums, which have attractive flowers
A is for alyssum with lovely honey fragrance
R is for roses and their beautiful scent
D is for daisies, delphiniums and dandelions
E is for Erica and white flowers lasting from winter to spring
N is for narcissus with ornamental flowers
S is for sunflowers, snowdrops and snapdragons.

Rachael Garnham (9)
Prettygate Junior School

Alphabet Food

(An extract A - I)

A is for apple red or green
B is for banana, which doesn't go with beans
C is for cake all sweet and jammy
D is for donut, which Sammy likes to eat
E is for egg that you eat on a seat
F is for fudge all sticky and gooey
G is for garlic, which you put in a stew
H is for ham that is as floppy as jelly
I is for . . .

Amy Louise Eavery (9)
Prettygate Junior School

Summer

Sunny bunnies come out to play
Sunny bunnies come in to stay
Sunny fairies come out to sing
Sunny fairies come in to rest
Rainy fairies come out to dance
Rainy fairies come in to prance
All of them come out to play
Then all of them come in to stay.

Rebecca Kelker (9)
Prettygate Junior School

In The Dark

In the dark I saw an owl
In the dark I heard a howl
In the forest I saw a bat
In the forest I felt a cat
In the castle I saw a ghost
In the castle I hit a post
And in the dark I saw a *monster!*

Jade Norris (8)
Prettygate Junior School

Lion Poem

Prowling, as it moves, preying on its prey
Trotting slowly through the grass

Gracefully getting ready to pounce

With its great mane as it's hiding in the pale
Long camouflaging itself

Then it takes the antelope by surprise

Growling like a legendary monster as it catches the antelope

Swiftly it pounces and bites.

Julian Chamberlain-Carter (10)
Prettygate Junior School

I Want To Be A . . .

I want to be a pop star
Singing on a stage

I want to be a painter
Painting on a page

I want to be a teacher
Teaching all the kids

I want to be a dustman
Banging with the lids.

Charlotte Emily Pincombe (8)
Prettygate Junior School

Crash Bash

Ten otters could be my nose
A sumo wrestler for my feet
I am taller than a double decker bus
An A3 sheet of paper for my ears
It's the sound of an asteroid
Crashing to Earth when I walk
A bent javelin beneath my nose
Could be my tusks
Can you guess what I am?

Joseph Daniels
Prettygate Junior School

Recipe For A Shark Sandwich

A shark sandwich is easy to make
All you do is simply take
One shark
Ten teeth
One sloppy tail
One onion ring
A dash of pepper
Some mayonnaise
Two bobby eyes
That ought to do it
And now comes the problem . . .
Biting into it!

Owen Pratt (8)
St James' CE Primary School

Recipe For A Strawberry And Cherry Sandwich

A strawberry and cherry sandwich is easy to make
All you do is simply take:
One slice of bread
One slice of cake
Some slimy jam
One juicy pepper
Some cherries and strawberries
One piece of ice cream
A dash of salt
That ought to do it
Now comes the problem
Biting into it!

Charlotte Phipps (8)
St James' CE Primary School

Recipe For A Cat Sandwich

A cat sandwich is easy to make
All you do is simply take
One slice of bread
A little bit of cat food
Some mayonnaise
Three cat's cake
One cat
A dash of pepper
That ought to do it
And now comes the problem . . .
Of biting into it!

Marissa Oshin
St James' CE Primary School

A Recipe For A Knuckle Sandwich

A knuckle sandwich is easy to make
All you do is simply take one slice of bread
One slice of cake
Some mayonnaise
One onion ring
One knuckle
One piece of string
A dash of pepper
That ought to do it
And now here comes the problem
Biting into it.

Adele Chumbley (8)
St James' CE Primary School

A Lion Sandwich

A lion sandwich is easy to make
All you do is simply take
One slice of bread
One slice of cake
Some mayonnaise
One scary lion
One piece of stretchy string
A dash of sneezy pepper
That ought to do it
And now comes the disgusting problem
Biting into the horrible sandwich.

Max Pope (8)
St James' CE Primary School

A Recipe For A Giraffe Sandwich

A giraffe sandwich is easy to make
All you do is simply take:
Two slices of bread
Two chunks of cake
Some tomato ketchup
One onion ring
One big giraffe
One metre of string
A dash of pepper
That must do it
Now comes the problem
Biting through it!

Melanie Dodds (8)
St James' CE Primary School

You're Not Going Out Like That

You're not going out like that
No way José
You're not going out like that
That skirt is a bit too short
You're not going out like that
You're falling off those heels
You're not going out like that
No way José you're not going out like that
N.O. spells no, you're not going out like that
Please Mum please Dad don't go out like that!

Chante Hunter (8)
St James' CE Primary School

Rules

Do not sit on paradise people
Do not jump on hopping hippos
Do not bathe in strawberry custard
Do not dance on singing tigers
Do not smoke on a snake's back
Do not take a lion to visit
Do not talk to a big bear
Do not lick a big lolly
Do not take a donkey's advice
To go to Daniel's sister's brother's house
And whatever else you do
It is better you do not!

Stefan King (8)
St James' CE Primary School

Humorous Poetry

A knuckle sandwich is easy
Just take some bread
A metal fist
A knuckle
A bone that is solid
A monkey brain
And an elephant
That ought to do it
Now here comes the problem
Biting into it!

Jack Benge (8)
St James' CE Primary School

Do Not . . .

Do not kick a donkey
Do not take a monkey's advice
Do not sit on a mushroom
Do not eat a monkey for breakfast
Do not sack an elephant from work
Do not take a camel to bed
Do not take some eggs to your mum
Do not have monkeys for dinner
Do not lick gum with your nose
Do not talk to four-headed people
Do not take a knuckle sandwich
Do not eat a purple goblin
Do not eat two-headed snakes
Do not eat a turkey fat ice cream
Do not kill your own parents
Do not take a witch's advice
Do not talk to big fat pigs
Do not take some pigs for breakfast
Do not jump in Barbie soup
Do not get some pigs and soup for breakfast
And whatever else you do do it is better you do not.

Daniel Higby (8)
St James' CE Primary School

Teacher Said

You can walk, slide, jog, slither, sneak, tiptoe
But don't run!

You can sprint, stealth, wander, dawdle, plod, zoom, dart
But don't run!

You can jump, skip, roll, gallop, crawl, creep, slink, glide
But don't run!

You can transport, sway, trundle, totter, trot, shuffle, stroll, and skate
But you don't run said my teacher
Then he ran.

Daniel Cutter (8)
St James' CE Primary School

A Recipe For An Elephant Sandwich

An elephant sandwich is easy to make
All you do is simply take:
Two slices of bread
A pack of crisps
Two jars of pepper
A giant clock
One table
Two elephants
One block of flats
One Titanic
Two hundred mice
Two spiders
A person's bottom
One giant's finger
Three piranhas
Two windows
A glass of milk
One shark
A cup of paintbrushes
Two plants
A tree
A flower
Two people
A baby elephant
Now comes the problem
Biting into it.

Joseph Austen (8)
St James' CE Primary School

Recipe For A Camel Cake

A camel cake is easy to make
All you do is simply take
Some sponge
A dash of cream
A camel a dash of salt
That is a big cake!
The problem is
Biting into it.

Georgia Aldous-Bland (8)
St James' CE Primary School

A Recipe For An Elephant Roll

An elephant roll is quite easy to make
All you do is always take
A piece of brown bread
One scraping of butter
Three pieces of wool and string
A clutter of pepper
To give it a taster
And add in some paste.

Amy Schilder (8)
St James' CE Primary School

Daydreaming

My mum thinks
I'm in the garden
Playing when I'm in
My bedroom dreaming
I'm a football player
Playing football in
The park.

Josh Madlin (9)
Suttons Primary School

Daydreaming

My dad thinks I'm reading
When really I'm a soldier
Trying to save my country
With a pistol on my shoulder

My mum thinks I'm Dracula
When really I'm in my vampire suit
But really I'm Frankenstein
With pumpkins all around me

My mum thinks I'm watching TV
When really I'm watching a DVD
But really I'm an astronaut
With the stars surrounding me.

Jack Driver (9)
Suttons Primary School

Daydreaming

My mum thinks I'm watching
TV when I'm really not
But really I'm a superhero

My mum thinks I'm sleeping
When I'm really not
Really I'm a fish swimming
In the sea with others

My mum thinks I'm doing
My homework when I'm not
But really I'm a monster
Roaring around the place.

Marc Minger (8)
Suttons Primary School

Daydreaming

My mum thinks I am
Tidying my room,
When I am not,
But really I am
Daydreaming,
With mermaids and
Fishes in my hair.

My dad thinks I'm going
To the shops,
But really I'm daydreaming,
On the beach,
With the seashells on
The seashore.

Tanya Jemal (9)
Suttons Primary School

Daydreaming

My mum thinks I'm
Doing my homework,
When I'm not,
I'm in space,
With an alien.

My mum thinks I'm
Reading,
When I'm not,
But really I am
On a rainbow,
Singing out loud.

Keenan O'Sullivan (8)
Suttons Primary School

Daydreaming

My mum thinks I'm asleep
When I'm in my bed,
But really I'm awake
With a spider on my head.

My nan thinks I'm hungry
When I'm looking for food,
But really I'm an inspector
Looking for clues.

Charlie Sandham (8)
Suttons Primary School

Daydreaming

My mum thinks I'm messing around,
When I'm in my bedroom,
But really I'm a monster,
In the house of doom.

My mum thinks I'm tidying my room,
It really is a mess,
But really I'm a glamour model,
Trying on a dress.

Emma Diggines (9)
Suttons Primary School

Daydreaming

My mum thinks I'm sleepy
When I'm really creepy,
But really I'm a superstar,
Slamming on my guitar.

My mum thinks I'm in bed,
When I'm really sharpening my lead,
But really I'm a ghost,
With the other's eating toast.

Melissa Kadir (7)
Suttons Primary School

Daydreaming

My mum thinks I'm a normal girl,
When I'm really a princess,
Just doing a twirl.

My brother thinks I adore him,
When I'm really trying to annoy him.

My mum thinks I'm playing in my room,
When I'm really lying on the floor,
But really I'm a mermaid eating more and more.

My mum thinks I'm sweeping,
When I'm really on my bed sleeping.

Nikki Eldridge (9)
Suttons Primary School

Daydreaming

My mum thinks I'm
Outside playing basketball.
When I have fun.
But really I'm playing my
Cool guitar with my best friend
Chelsea.

Sarah Blyth (8)
Suttons Primary School

Dog Daydream Poem

My mum thinks I'm sleeping,
But really I'm daydreaming, of a dog,
Behind a tree peeping,
At me chewing a log.

Matthew Hayes (8)
Suttons Primary School

Daydreaming

My mum thinks I'm reading
A school book,
When really I'm bored,
But really I'm on a beach.

My dad thinks,
I'm eating my dinner,
When really I'm a superstar.

My nan thinks I'm playing
In the garden,
When really I'm a sports woman,
Running a race.

Ceri Frost (9)
Suttons Primary School

Daydreaming

My dog thinks I'm playful,
When we're in the park,
But really I'm a shark,
With razor sharp teeth.

My chip thinks I'm cod in batter,
When I'm on the sofa,
But really I'm Donkeykong
With my mate Godzilla.

My alien thinks I'm a hamster
When I eat cheesy nibbles,
But really I'm a learner,
With a racing car.

Laurence Few (9)
Suttons Primary School

Bare Tree

Boring, old, bare tree,
Really ugly now,
Wind is gathering speed,
Creaking every bough.

Boring, old, bare tree,
Sitting in the park,
Lightening struck the old tree,
And left a nasty mark.

Boring, old, bare tree,
All its leaves are lost,
Maybe tomorrow morning,
It'll be covered in frost.

Boring, old, bare tree,
Waiting for spring to come,
Birds sitting in the tree,
Singing a beautiful hum.

Boring, old, bare tree,
A very dark and dull brown,
Some of the drivers look at it,
While driving into town.

Boring, old, bare tree,
Is no longer boring and old,
As spring is coming now,
It is no longer cold.

Boring, old, bare tree,
Having so much fun,
No longer old and boring,
Instead shining in the sun.

Harry Offord (11)
Suttons Primary School

The Rocket That Philip Built

This is the rocket that Philip built.

This is the food,
That was put on the rocket that Philip built.

This is the mouse,
That ate the food,
That was put on the rocket that Philip built.

This is the dog that
Scared the mouse,
That ate the food,
That was put on the rocket that Philip built.

This is the pound that,
Worried the dog that,
Scared the mouse,
That ate the food,
That was put on the rocket that Philip built.

Philip Hayes
Suttons Primary School

Favourite Things

Secret places,
Secret things
Secret friends
Hidden carefully, out of sight.
My favourite things like:
The taste of chocolate,
The smell of fish and chips,
The sound of a baby's laughter,
The touch of a silky red rose,
The sight of the red hot sun.

Samantha O'Donoghue (11)
Suttons Primary School

My New Shoes

My new shoes are too big
For me to wear
They're nice to wear anywhere
I will always go out in them.

My new shoes have to be worn
Indoors I like my shoes
They are fashionable.

My new shoes will go everywhere
They'll go up, they'll go down or anywhere
They'll go right around.

My shoes are comfortable
Even when we're at the table,
I will always be able
To eat my dinner at the table
In my new shoes.

Thomas Freeman (9)
Suttons Primary School

The Door Marked Private

The forbidden gate was marked with private
I dare not pass
The thoughts that rush through my mind
Of a sharp cage
Afraid and scared are my thoughts
A killer animal might be contained
To pounce on me
And use its claws
To scratch my flesh
For red liquid to run from my veins
To its mouth.

Joanne Hardy (11)
Suttons Primary School

The School That Charlie Built

This is the school that Charlie built.

This is the desk,
That stood in the school that Charlie built.

These are the children
That sat at the desks
That stood in the school that Charlie built.

This is the teacher
That taught the children
That sat at the desks
That stood in the school that Charlie built.

This is the dog
That scared the teacher
That taught the children
That sat at the desks
That stood in the school that Charlie built.

This is the fox
That frightened the dog
That scared the teacher
That taught the children
That sat at the desks
That stood in the school that Charlie built.

Kirsty Horridge (11)
Suttons Primary School

Dream Poem

I dreamed I was riding a dog,
Who jumped over a big brown log,
He jumped so high he touched the sky,
That's why I love my furry brown dog.

Hannah Stracey (9)
Suttons Primary School

The Tortoise

The tortoise is a sleepy animal
And very slow,
But the tortoise is affected
By autumn a lot.

Packed up in a box
The tortoise lay
With nothing to do or say.

The tortoise lay
Still and weary
With no reason to be.

Eventually the time will come for the
Tortoise to be released
And free.

But until then
The tortoise
Lay still and weary
With no reason to be.

Tommy Wells–Bolger (10)
Suttons Primary School

Bare Tree

Tall trees lurk upon the sky
Nature's gift planted so high

Bare trees wet and damp with rainfall to come

Cold as winter, freezing as spring
Bare trees is what they bring

Dark or bright. They need no light
Bare trees stay out at night.

Michael Nugent (10)
Suttons Primary School

Foot

This is the foot that helps me kick.

This is the ball,
That the foot kicked.

This is the goal,
That the ball went in,
That the foot kicked.

This is the goalie,
That stands in the goal,
That the ball went in,
That the foot kicked.

This is the end of the game,
The goalie's gone home,
The goal is empty,
The ball has gone,
And the foot is still working.

Laura North (10)
Suttons Primary School

Night

A big, black blanket in the sky
Way up, higher than high
Tuck up tight
Getting ready for the night

You have had a wonderful day
Mum comes up to say

Night! Night!
Sleep light
Have a lovely dream tonight.

Megan Rogers (11)
Suttons Primary School

Imagine

Imagine there's no colour,
Everything was black and white,
There weren't any decorations,
And there wasn't any light.

Imagine if the world was gold,
And the sky wasn't blue,
Imagine if we lived outside,
And only wore one shoe.

Imagine there's no death,
No one would risk their life,
No soldiers would be dead,
And no one would be killed with a knife.

Imagine the world was empty,
The only person was me,
There was no one to have fun with,
And there were no insects like a bee.

Imagine all the things been said,
Some things are good and bad,
Some things are really happy,
And some things are really sad.

Nicola Horridge (10)
Suttons Primary School

Imagine

Imagine there was no light,
No one would be able to see,
The sun, the moon and the lampposts,
Gives you light indeed.

Cherise O'Sullivan (11)
Suttons Primary School

This Is The Cat

This is the cat.

This is the cat
That lay on the mat.

This is the cat
That lay on the mat
That is very fat.

This is the cat
That lay on the mat
That is very fat
That squashed the rat.

This is the cat
That lay on the mat
That is very fat
That squashed the rat
That is very flat.

Jessica Harrison (11)
Suttons Primary School

New Shoes

When you're walking down the
Street with your comfortable
Feet you could run you
Could walk and sprint with
Your comfortable feet

When you're walking down
The street with your
Comfortable feet you could
Go to a party with
Your new shoes!

George Ebert (10)
Suttons Primary School

No Name

No names for people
Or any other thing
No one to call out to
But do not stop rejoicing.

All you can shout out is 'hey'
No one you can call for help
No one to call out to
Why you sit there and yelp.

No one can bully you
They cannot call you names
No one to call out to
Calling you all different things
While you think they're playing games.

No name on you death stone
Only RIP
No one to call out to
God only knows your name.

Tommy Unwin (10)
Suttons Primary School

Cats Are Just Cats

Playful cats,
Sleepy cats,
Cats are sometimes lazy,
They sit there all day
Which they do a lot
But they are very loving
Just remember cats are just cats.

Amy Chessher (10)
Suttons Primary School

Football

This is the foot
That had the boot.

This is the foot
That had the boot
That kicked the ball.

This is the foot,
That had the boot,
That kicked the ball,
That scored a goal for
England.

This is the foot,
That had the boot,
That kicked the ball,
That scored a goal for
England
That made them win the
World Cup.

Carl Harrison (11)
Suttons Primary School

I Dreamt I Was Riding A Cat

I dreamt I was riding a cat with
A yellow golden mat
He sat and sat on the mat
Then he wanted a pat
Mog saw a rat
Then he licked the rat
He put on the hat
There was a bat in the hat
Mog ate the rat
Then he felt fat.

Siân O'Sullivan (7)
Suttons Primary School

Imagine

Imagine there are no people
Everywhere you go
Silence all around you
No one to know
The world is cold and silent
You look around to see
No one standing round you
Only me

Imagine there's no peace
Hunger and depressed
Everyone is fighting
All around me war
And the cold hands of death
But yet hope lives in all

Imagine no world at all
A place of darkness
Nothing, empty, no life
Dark, damp, died, died, died.

Amy Sands (10)
Suttons Primary School

The Alien

Lives in a mother ship, long but skinny
Scary, freaky, nasty and weak
Never seen by the human eye before then
He creeps down his mother ship
Waiting and waiting for people to arrive
With his big eyes he stalks to abduct

He wears nothing, his feet are small
And his head is big.

Lewis Rix (11)
Suttons Primary School

Imagine

Imagine having no sunshine
No warmth for us to enjoy

Imagine there being no fights
The peace we'd have would be good

Imagine no home to run to
When we are in need of one

Imagine having no music
Not a sound we can enjoy

Imagine having no parents
No one we can then hug

These things we expect to be here
So we're amused and we're loved.

Demi Mills (10)
Suttons Primary School

So Many Faces

So many faces, in one little world
Where did they come from?

So many feelings in one little world
What do they mean?

So many actions in one little world
Where did they begin?

So many questions, in one little world
Where are the answers?

Jessica Samuel (10)
Suttons Primary School

Imagine

Imagine there was no fighting
Everybody lived in peace
There were no wars
Just happiness
Imagine all the people that get hurt
Just through fighting

Imagine there was no bullying
No one's feelings ever got hurt
No one was spiteful
Just kindness
Imagine all the people that are offended
Just through bullying

Imagine there was no kindness
No one ever felt proud
No one felt good about helping anyone
Just nastiness
Imagine all the people that are happy
Just through kindness
Kindness.

Billie Kennerson (11)
Suttons Primary School

I Dreamed I Was Riding A Hare

I dreamed I was riding a hare
I took him to the fair
He looked like Tony Blair
And got married to the mayor
And everyone was in front of him
All sitting on chairs
And everyone cares for him
He's the new Tony Blair.

Toby Moore (8)
Suttons Primary School

Imagine

Imagine no mums
No one there to
Talk to about your fears.

Imagine no transport
No one will be driving
Just walking.

Imagine no animals
Nothing to look at
No fun.

Imagine no people
No one there
No one there.

Imagine no nose
Wouldn't be able to smell
Plain plain.

Imagine no holidays
No planes no flying.

Imagine no
Face
Imagine.

Aaron Parsons (9)
Suttons Primary School

A Bridge

Bridge, bridge in the sky you are sweeter
Than a piece of pie, it makes me want to fly
Boat, boat, going by, with light as ever
Silent, like a prayer
Bridge, bridge everywhere.

Alfie Ryan (10)
Suttons Primary School

I Dreamed I Was Riding A Dog

I dreamed I was riding a dog
On a log
And there I saw a frog
In the river
It was very strange because
The dog ate the frog
And the log
Such a funny dream
I have ever seen.

Sophie Jenkins (8)
Suttons Primary School

My Dream Poem

My mum thinks I'm
Sleeping but really I'm eating
Bugs and slugs and all different
Kinds of insect. I take them
To school and show Mrs
Butler and all she does is run
Down the hall.

Georgia Smith (9)
Suttons Primary School

Dream Poem

I dreamed I was riding a cat
Who was very fat and wore a hat
When I woke up it turned into a rat
I showed the wizard's bat my cat
Then I showed a tiny gnat my cat
Who turned into a rat.

Rebecca Green (9)
Suttons Primary School

Voices

Scary, strange or squeaky
They give you all a fright
Loud or quiet
High or low
Voices everywhere

When you hear a whisper
You turn around with a shock
Sounding like a ghost
So spooky
Voices everywhere

Suddenly you hear a scream
What's going on?
Who's there you think
You're puzzled
Voices everywhere

A shout in your left ear
A howl in your right
Boo, comes out of the darkness
Roar, from the opposite side
Voices, such a scare.

Luke Abrahams (11)
Suttons Primary School

My Dream Poem

My football trainer thinks I'm training
But really I'm in Paris when it's raining
My dad thinks I'm in a stare
But really I'm like Mr Tony Blair
My mum thinks I'm playing golf
But really I'm the new Rudolph
My sister thinks I'm in a different land
But really I'm in Eminem's band.

Lewis Winters (7)
Suttons Primary School

Voices

Loud voices, quiet voices
Deep voices, soft voices
Girls and boys voices
People sound different

Babies screaming, children crying
Dads shouting, mums whispering
Old ladies moaning, granddads groaning
People sound different

There are scary voices
Funny voices, nice voices
Strange voices
People sound different

Some people have
Squeaky voices
Others hardly speak
People sound different.

Kailey Bickmore (9)
Suttons Primary School

Daydreaming

My dad thinks I'm mad
When I'm jumping around
But really I'm Superman
With can in my hand

My brother thinks I'm crazy
When I say 'Boom boom'
But really I'm Basil Brush
With an elephant in my room.

Billy Markham (9)
Suttons Primary School

Night Is Here

The moon is shining
People are going out
The stars are shining like glitter

Now it is pitch black
People getting scared
But the moon is shining beautifully
So there's a little bit of light

People going home at night
People getting frightened
Stars shining like a flashlight

Now children are in bed
Adults watching telly
Now it is bedtime
And morning will come.

Rebecca Boyce (9)
Suttons Primary School

Daydreaming

My mum thinks I'm
Jumping on my bed
But I'm really a lady
With a surfboard surfing
On the waves
On the sea

My mum thinks I'm reading
But I wasn't I was
Jumping on my bed
Instead

My mum thinks I'm
Doing my room but
I'm really a puppy
Catching my ball.

Bethan Gully (7)
Suttons Primary School

Doing Favourite Things

Having fun playing
All day, don't
Stop playing until
The day ends.

Playing football
Having fun, don't
Stop running
Just run, run, run.

Being happy, not sad
When you play football
Just go mad.

Going out shopping to
Get some sweets
I love going out
To eat, eat, eat.

After that I
Got to bed
But when Mum's
Sleeping I play instead.

Anthony Martin (11)
Suttons Primary School

Jelly And Ice Cream

Wibble, wobble, wibble
Jelly makes you dribble.

Have a nice dream
About ice cream.

Let the jelly
Get in your belly.

Then go to the stream
And have an ice cream.

Clara-Jane Edwards (10)
Suttons Primary School

Voices

Candle lit, flame burning in
The marble church
The person's voice, echoing
Getting louder, louder and then. Softer.

James Coburn (10)
Suttons Primary School

Daydream

My mum thinks I'm going to town
But really I'm buying a clown
It's really weird
Because it's got a crown and a beard.

Sophie Andrews (8)
Suttons Primary School

I Dreamed I Was Riding A Cat

I dreamed I was riding a cat
With a little tiny red hat
He was a very fat cat
And he always sat on his mat.

Ellie Noble (8)
Suttons Primary School

Monster Me

My dad thinks I'm asleep when my eyes
Are closed up tight but really I'm a
Monster with a big appetite.

Michael Wilks (9)
Suttons Primary School

Imagine

Imagine there were no God
Surely you could if you tried
No world around us
There wouldn't be any people
Imagine all the world
Dark and naked

Imagine there were no villains
Surely you could
All the people smiling cause they're safe
No one will die
So painful
Imagine all the people smiling
Because they're safe

Imagine if there was no electricity
You can I'm sure
No TV no light
Quiet and dark
Imagine all the people
Living in boredom

Imagine if there were no police
You can really, try your hardest
6000 murders every day
No punishment will be given
Imagine the whole wide world
Living unsafe

People tell me stop day dreaming
But it's true

Imagine how the world would run like this.

Meg Barry (9)
Suttons Primary School

Working Man's Work

On the Monday morning the cleaners come to call
He was cleaning the windows
The window broke and he had a fall
We had to call a glazer
And it's more work to do

On the Tuesday morning the glazer came to call
He was fixing the window
But he fell from the ladder
And we had to call an ambulance
And it's much more work to do

On the Wednesday morning the ambulance came to call
But the ambulance broke down
So it was no good at all
We had to call a mechanic
And it's more work to do

On the Thursday morning the mechanic came to call
It was going fine
When the tyres burst
We had to get a tyre fitter
But it's just more work to do

On the Friday morning a tyre fitter came to call
The tyres were pumping up perfectly
Suddenly his spanner slipped and cracked a window
Now it's more work to do

On a Saturday morning the glazer came to call
He had no glass so he boarded up the window
He left wood shavings on the floor
And it's more work to do.

Samuel Webster (9)
Suttons Primary School

Prowling

When cats go prowling in the darkness
You'll never know when they'll return
Their shadow silhouette in the moonlight
Their eyes' glowing ready to pounce.

When cats laze around
They'll be expecting to sleep all day
So if you take them in to the tub
They'll certainly kick and scratch.

When cats go out for fun
They end up killing birds
Dragging them into the living room
It'll frighten your sister and maker her run.

Jade Carey (10)
Suttons Primary School

The Grimy Bridge

The grimy bridge,
Mouldy and dirty,
Looks the age of one hundred and thirty.

The old bridge,
Crusty and grimy,
Look at it,
It's so slimy.

The slimy bridge
With bricks falling out
The only person who sits there is a
Lager lout.

Joe O'Neill (11)
Suttons Primary School

Imagine

Imagine there's no school
No children happy
No lessons
No fun
Just imagine it now.

Imagine there's no dancing
No laughter as they jump
No music
No spinning
Just imagine it now.

Imagine there's no electricity
No acting on TV
No computers working
No music playing
Just imagine it now.

Jessica Irvine (9)
Suttons Primary School

Imagine

Imagine there's no electricity
It's hard, It's tough
There's no cars or light
Which makes us really rough.

Imagine you get lost
And you're scared out of your bones
You want to run away
But you decide to stay.

Imagine great things
Like wanting to sing
Be something you want to be
Make your dream come true
I believe in you.

Michaela Black (11)
Suttons Primary School

Cats

Some cats are fat
Some cats are thin
Some look for fish in bins
Cats

Some people pat cats
Children cuddle cats
And cats will catch rats
Cats

Cats are all different
Black, ginger or even brown
Some cats live in town
Cats

Cats have kittens
Some big, some small
Once they've finished eating
They will say miaow, 'I'm done'
Cats.

Amber Edwards (11)
Suttons Primary School

Mud

Mud is slippery,
Mud is dirty,
Mud is big and small.

Mud is wet,
Mud is brown,
All over the ground.

Puddles of mud,
Streams of mud,
Lakes of mud.

But I like mud as it is.

Jack Litson (9)
Suttons Primary School

The House That Jim Built

This is the house that Jim built

This is the sofa
That stays in the house that Jim built.

This is the mum
That sits on the sofa
That stays in the house that Jim built.

This is the dad
That kisses the mum
That sits on the sofa
That stays in the house that Jim built.

This is the garden
That was built by the dad
That kisses the mum
That sits on the sofa
That stays in the house that Jim built.

This is the grass
That lays in the garden
That was built by the dad
That kisses the mum
That sits on the sofa
That stays in the house that Jim built.

George Weller (10)
Suttons Primary School

I Dreamed That I Was On A Leopard

I dreamed that I was on a leopard
They have big great claws and big great paws

And a very spotty coat, he took me to the zoo
Then he threw me in a large shoe.

Abbie Middleditch (9)
Suttons Primary School

That's What Happens At Night

The whispers in the trees,
Caused by the slight breeze
The shadowed sky, with the full moon
Gives some people a fright
That's what happens at night.

The dark blue moonlit night
Beautiful, but not for some
People imagine the ghosts come
That's what happens at night.

Now the night is thinning
The morning birds are singing
The sun comes up over the trees
Now the night is over.

Molly Adams (9)
Suttons Primary School